The
ULTIMATE
RANDOM
ENCOUNTERS
—— BOOK ——

The
ULTIMATE RANDOM ENCOUNTERS
BOOK

Hundreds of Original Encounters
to Help Bring Your Next
RPG Adventure to Life

Travis "Wheels" Wheeler, Logan Jenkins,
Lee Terrill, and Greg Leatherman

ADAMS MEDIA
NEW YORK   LONDON   TORONTO   SYDNEY   NEW DELHI

Adams Media
An Imprint of Simon & Schuster, Inc.
100 Technology Center Drive
Stoughton, Massachusetts 02072

First Adams Media trade paperback edition October 2021

ADAMS MEDIA and colophon are trademarks of Simon & Schuster.

For information about special discounts for bulk purchases, please contact Simon & Schuster Special Sales at 1-866-506-1949 or business@simonandschuster.com.

The Simon & Schuster Speakers Bureau can bring authors to your live event. For more information or to book an event contact the Simon & Schuster Speakers Bureau at 1-866-248-3049 or visit our website at www.simonspeakers.com.

Interior design by Julia Jacintho
Illustrations by Cinthia Rashford, Rob Donovan, and Priscilla Yuen

Manufactured in China

10 9 8 7 6 5 4

Library of Congress Cataloging-in-Publication Data
Names: Wheeler, Travis, author. | Jenkins, Logan, author. | Terrill, Lee, author. | Leatherman, Greg, author.
Title: The ultimate random encounters book / Travis "Wheels" Wheeler, Logan Jenkins, Lee Terrill, and Greg Leatherman.
Other titles: Hundreds of original encounters to help bring your next role playing game adventure to life
Description: First Adams Media Trade Paperback Edition. | Stoughton, Massachusetts: Adams Media, 2021. | "Illustrations by Cinthia Rashford and Rob Donovan"--T.p. verso.
Identifiers: LCCN 2021005948 | ISBN 9781507216378 (pb) | ISBN 9781507216385 (eBook)
Subjects: LCSH: Fantasy games--Handbooks, manuals, etc. | Role playing.
Classification: LCC GV1469.6 .W436 2021 | DDC 793.93--dc23
LC record available at https://lccn.loc.gov/2021005948

ISBN 978-1-5072-1637-8
ISBN 978-1-5072-1638-5 (ebook)

CONTENTS

INTRODUCTION

Playing a role-playing game is a delicate dance. If everything runs smoothly, it feels like you and your friends are able to maneuver effortlessly through dramatic, epic, and uproariously silly scenes where everyone gets a chance to shine.

And yet, other times it just doesn't come together. Combat slows to a repetitive grind, the game master runs out of good non-player character (NPC) ideas, or after twenty-six rounds maybe even the most beautifully designed encounter just gets a bit stale.

Sure, you *could* prep an absolute powerhouse of an all-killer, no-filler role-playing session. Spend time getting fun character voices ready for every NPC. Map out a bunch of separate combat encounters. Intricately weave a tale of beauty and sorrow.

But that sounds like *way* too much work. Plus, most games put all that responsibility on the GM alone; someone is going to be saddled with a ton of homework just so you can all play every other Tuesday.

This is the book you turn to for help. It's a big book of ideas designed to slot right into your existing campaign, organized into neat little tables.

Got a pre-existing world but you're running dry on things to have the party do in it? Flip to Part 1 and roll up one of our random encounters.

Got the rough sketches of an encounter but not time enough to populate every nook and cranny of the setting? No problem. Prep as much as you can and fill in the rest from the game master tools in Part 2.

If you salivate at chaos magic effect tables and daydream about wild, unexpected die results, you already know it can also be fun to throw caution to the wind and let randomness determine as much as possible. Even the most organized GMs and the tightest adventure modules benefit from a little spice!

BECOME ONE WITH THE DICE

Once you get enough practice with it, using random generation can vastly enhance your game. Even with minimal prep, your table flows with novel ideas, unpredictable stories, and happy narrative accidents.

Getting to that point can take some mindset shifts though. It's just as easy to roll up some random elements, stare in bafflement at what the table gave you, and give up entirely. Thankfully, though, all it takes to get going again is another roll on the table.

Randomly selected elements from tables like the ones in this book are entirely disposable. If you roll up an encounter, read it, and it doesn't sing to you, take a note from Marie Kondo: Throw it out and roll again until you read one that sparks joy.

That goes for individual elements too. Many encounters in this book are written with a lot of flashy elements that you can sculpt down into the perfect session for your group. If the encounter features a werewolf ex-paladin mercenary, maybe you ditch the "mercenary" detail because you fought mercenaries last week.

Once you've mastered the reroll and the substitution techniques, you'll find the random elements from your sessions feel like you planned them on your own. They'll fit your story like a glove, because you've already got incredible ideas. Randomization provides you the sandbox in which to use them.

HOW DO I USE THIS BOOK?

There are two approaches to using the random tables in this book.

First, the GM can roll some random elements in advance to speed up preparation time. Implement your best ideas, then turn to this book for the small details, like NPC motivations or random encounters, to fill the gaps between points of interest.

Second, you can rely on this book for complete pickup RPG sessions. Maybe you've got half your normal group over. You can't exactly pick up where you left off in the story without the rest of the group. Whip out this book, roll a random encounter, and you've got yourself a session that requires zero prep and that doesn't need to advance your pre-existing plot. The resulting Franken-session of random NPCs, encounters, and settings will probably be a bit odd, but you've already got a handful of creative minds at the table who can help you make sense of what you wind up with.

This book is split into three parts: Part 1 contains nine tables based on game environments from which you can generate random encounters for your characters. Part 2 features tools for game masters looking to tweak game details. Part 3 lists various downtime encounters you can use in any game to flesh out characters' personalities and have some fun group banter.

USING PART ONE: ENCOUNTER TABLES

The encounter tables of Part 1 are the biggest chunk of the book, since random encounters save you the most time in prep.

While you might think of a combat opportunity when you hear "encounter," an encounter can really be any event that hooks the players into role-play or strategy or both! This book's encounters run the gamut from nail-biting brawls to relaxing comedic romps with oddball NPCs.

Simply flip to the section for the environment the party is in, then use any method of picking a random number between 1 and 100. Two d10s work great. You can also just read through a few pages' worth of encounters ahead of time and pick one that stands out to you. In each section you'll find maps that illustrate some of the encounters. Those encounters that take place in the mapped locations have their numbers circled for easy identification.

The encounter will give you more than enough ideas to get started. If you want, you can add or remove elements of your own to tweak the session to fit what you think your group will enjoy best.

USING PART TWO: GM TOOLS

If the encounters of Part 1 are the meat and potatoes of your next RPG session, the GM tools of Part 2 are the sides and sauces that bring it all together.

You can use these tables to add motivation to existing characters, generate entirely new NPCs, quickly whip together new locations, or even provide wild mid-encounter twists to keep the players on their toes.

USING PART THREE: DOWNTIME

Part 3 contains encounters that are fit for anywhere in your adventure and not tied to a specific location.

But enough talk. Let's get down to it!

9

PART ONE

ENCOUNTERS

The encounter prompts in this book are grouped into tables by setting, with one hundred encounters per table.

If you're trying to insert these encounters into a pre-existing campaign, good news: Just pick the table whose setting fits the story you're in the middle of, and play encounters from there until you want a change of scenery. If you're starting from scratch, good news: You get your pick of the litter. Each table begins with an introductory section that explains what kind of adventures you can expect from the setting. Choose whichever one sounds best to your group.

From there you can either select the encounters that stick out to you or choose a number between 1 and 100 to let chance decide.

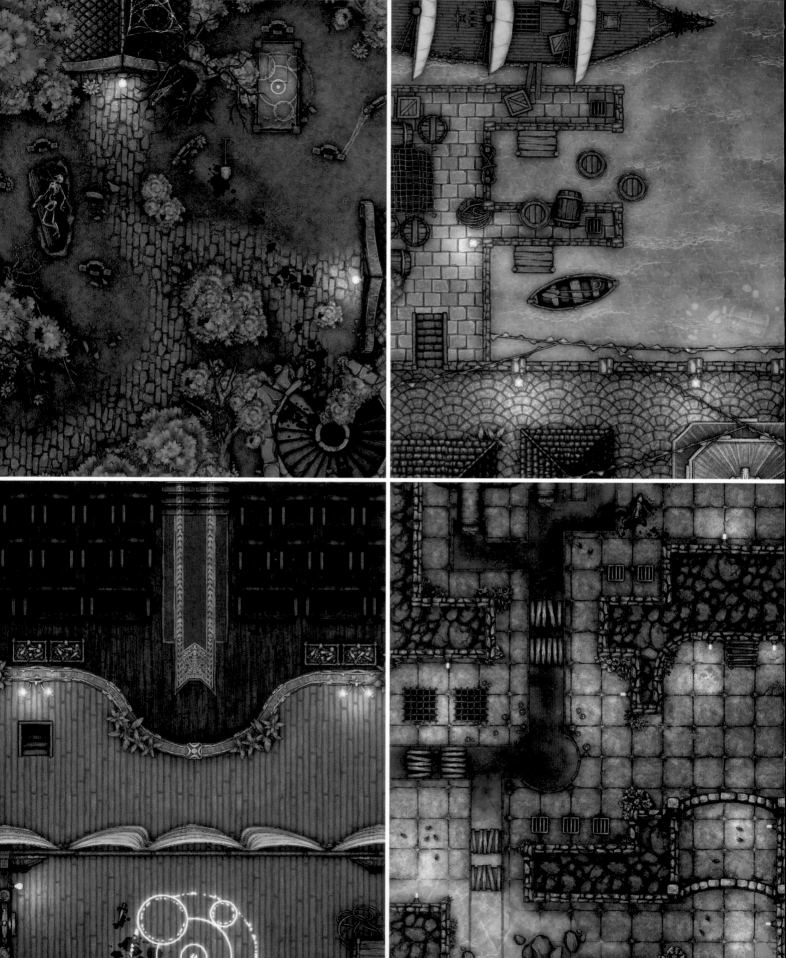

CITY

Welcome to the city! Just like metropolitan areas in real life, fictional cities are the places where a community's hidden contradictions start to show. Poor areas ravaged by crime syndicates rest within spitting distance of rich socialites frittering away wealth. Royals and rebels vie for turf. Mass disasters roll in alongside tiny, personal disputes.

On the lighter side, cities are stuffed with the most interesting creature in any RPG setting—people! For this reason, cities are great settings for players in your group who will never shirk a chance to perform, who are interested in fantasy fashion, or who are always in search of a new friend.

1 A bounty hunter has come looking for an elf wanted dead or alive. The elf is a member of the city council and must be protected at all costs. The bounty hunter only attacks at night.

2 A troupe of gnomish inventors has taken over an abandoned warehouse on the pier and has been there for months. No one knew they were there until the loud noises and strange smells started. Now they claim they own the building and have five war machines to defend their home.

3 One of the town guards swears that he was bitten by a werewolf and has asked the heroes to help him. The full moon is in two days, and the guard is known to tell lies on a regular basis.

4 A spell has accidentally gone off in the city's library, animating all the books. The books are now attacking patrons. The library needs help, but the books are too valuable to destroy!

5 An evil librarian has hidden five books in the city library that will drive anyone who reads them mad. Finding the books will be no easy task.

6 A member of your group accidentally runs into a stranger; the collision sends a pendant shattering to the ground. At this moment, the two characters swap bodies. The annoyed stranger explains the effect will wear off in twenty-four hours but demands compensation for their broken artifact.

7 The players are approached by a young person claiming to be a big fan interested in helping with the adventure. They have made crude fan art of the characters.

8 There's a murder in town, and the players are the guards' first suspects. After all, they were within a block of the crime scene, and every one of them is kitted out with horrifying weapons.

9 A noble unexpectedly invites the players to a two-day event to celebrate the upcoming holiday. It turns out the father wishes to teach his son how to survive in the "real world" and wants the players to hunt his son on their grounds for the next two days. The pay is considerable.

10 A songbird keeps bugging the players. If anyone can translate, the bird tells the story of a poor prince locked away in his room. He desperately needs to be rescued lest he be married off to his third cousin.

11 A thief steals one of the player's sentimental or magical items. The thief then shape-shifts into a dog and hides by joining a pack of stray dogs. Can the players figure out which dogs are real, and which one just stole their things?

12 A ramshackle tenement building the players rest in crumbles entirely while dozens of people are inside. The slumlord has no intention of finding new housing for the residents of the tenement, nor for travelers, like the players, staying there.

13 The villain (or make a new one if you don't already have one!) sends henchmen to build an ugly billboard to improve their own image, and they've done so at a sacred historical site of sentimental value to the players or to an NPC they admire.

14 The city is holding a magical battle of the bands. Emphasis on "battle."

15 A figure in a lumpy gray cloak is conducting magically animated objects to construct a building. They introduce themself as the Wodgian Wizard of the Walls. Unfortunately, the animated objects won't stop construction. For them to stop, they must be broken. If the players help, the wizard offers a card with their picture on it. This spell card can animate household objects to perform a task.

16 The tavern is stuck in a time loop! The players have one minute before the loop restarts. A deal has gone wrong in a back room, resulting in a magical crystal shattering, messing with time in the immediate area.

17 The monument in the center of town cracks open and an ancient being bursts out. It seems they were petrified one thousand years ago and everyone forgot! They need a guide to this new, vastly different life.

18 The city is hosting its annual Tournament of Champions: a no-holds-barred freestyle combat competition where contestants fight to the "death." Fortunately, a death ward is placed on the participants so that their death only eliminates them from the tournament. There is a huge prize for first place!

19 One of the players is confronted by someone they've done harm to in the past. How do the others react upon learning about this misdeed? How does the confronted player treat the individual?

20 The players feel a slight jostle, then see a group of small figures running away from them. Checking their belongings, they realize their money is gone! They can barely see the figures running away in the distance.

21 The circus is in town, and there's a giant bounty on the clown's head.

22 An advisor to the king has hired the players to kill a party of assassins from a rival nation that are rumored to be coming to kill the king. However, the "assassins" are actually diplomats and the advisor is looking to start a war.

23 It's been snowing on the castle, and only the castle, for three days now. Everyone will be trapped inside unless the source of the storm can be found and stopped.

24 A nobleman hires the players as guards to make sure he and his friends are safe while they tour and take stock of the poor section of town. It's clear they just want to gawk at the poor.

25 A local tavern, The Wayward Boy, has become wildly popular, attracting world-class bards. A rival business owner started a rumor that the tavern is run by two incubi and offers to hire the players to attack the popular tavern. In reality, the tavern is run by two retired male adventurers in love.

26 The king has died with no clear line of succession. Two sets of families are fighting for control. It is said that the king left a will stating his wishes, but no one can seem to find it. One of the families hires the players to help them look.

27 The gargoyles on the church have been replaced by real gargoyles that come to life at night and have been terrorizing the city.

28 A trio of grave robbers is searching for treasure from the tombs of the rich. The players must stop these fools before they accidently unleash a greater evil that has been bound within a massive family tomb.

29 A merchant wants to buy a store on the main square but believes it is haunted. She needs someone to check it out and get rid of the ghosts. The players find that the "ghosts" are really a rival store owner using mercenaries to scare competition away from the location.

30 The cemetery and the catacombs beneath are warded against anyone raising the bodies as undead, but the caretaker believes the wards have been tampered with. The players must find out who is weakening the wards before they bring forth an army of the undead.

31 A gnomish inventor needs help setting up his booth to sell trinkets at the harvest festival. He leaves out the part about how explosive and unpredictable some of his new items are.

32 The young daughter of a family of wizards has run off. The family doesn't know why and wants her found. She is hiding in the graveyard because she wants to be a necromancer.

33 The minotaur run is an annual event in the city. Those who wish to participate must navigate a maze that takes up the entire central marketplace while running away from the minotaurs.

34 A local gang has taken the head of the merchants guild hostage. Unless their demands are met, they plan on killing him. They demand that the city watch leave the area and state that they have a list of demands that they will only give to a neutral party.

35 A water spirit has become trapped in the central fountain. All anyone knows is that the water in the fountain isn't acting normal and seems to have a mind of its own.

36 Deep within the cemetery, in a sealed tomb, a cult finally has all of what it needs to summon forth an ancient evil. The groundskeepers have been kidnapped to be sacrificed upon this evil's awakening.

37 The city is hosting an apple festival with promises of prizes for those who compete and win in the various contests. The team with the most points at the end of the festival wins 50 gold. Events include pie eating, apple crushing, apple tossing, and trivia about local apples.

38 A guild war has been escalating, and now the thieves guild has kidnapped the head of the merchants guild and buried her alive in the cemetery. The players need to find her fast, as well as deal with the thieves guild lackey left on guard duty in the cemetery.

39 Parts of the central marketplace have collapsed into sinkholes. A huge burrowing mole has decided to take up residence beneath the city market and has weakened large swathes of land all over town. This mole has got to go.

40 All the tapestries in the throne room have changed and now depict fire raining from the sky. Are they showing what is to come, or is this a trick meant to scare the kingdom?

41 Random merchants have been falling suddenly ill and slipping into a coma right at their stalls. A cursed coin has been planted in the marketplace and affects any merchant who touches it.

42 The head of the fishing guild secretly withholds their portion of the offerings made each spring to appease the sea. Enraged at this slight, sea spirits begin attacking the town. The players must find a way to stop the spirits from destroying the city.

43 The players have been hired as extra security at the prince's coronation. The prince, who is about to be crowned king, is a fake. The real prince has been cursed and is trying to stop his evil counterpart.

44 A quartet of singing ghosts always starts off the city's harvest festival. This year, they fail to manifest! The players must find the villain, who has captured the ghosts in spirit jars, among the angry and confused festivalgoers.

45 A master thief has stolen a priceless artifact from the local temple and is attempting to escape by sea. The players need to find the thief and the artifact, and deal with the thief's goons, who are lying in ambush at the pier.

46 Pickpockets have been plaguing the central market for weeks, and the council is at wits' end. They want the players to end the problem one way...or another.

47 The king and queen have had a child, and everyone is here to give their blessings. But an evil warlock plans to curse the child unless he can be stopped.

48 The local governor believes that pirates are moving monstrous animals through the port of this city and she wants it stopped. The pirates have, fortunately, gotten careless with hiding the contraband animals. But now the players must stop the pirates and corral their most recent monster...a large chimera.

49 A king's advisor had a startling dream about the princess disappearing and saw the players in that dream. The players are summoned before the advisor to answer for a crime that hasn't happened yet.

50 A group called Ocean's 5 has hired undersea elves to tamper with a fishing tournament and ensure their win. Other participants suspect this group is cheating but can't tell how. Can the players find out how Ocean's 5 is winning everything before people take matters into their own hands?

51 All the doors in the castle no longer lead to their correct rooms. The king's advisor thinks a recently captured orb may be the source of this space warping. The players must try to reach the orb despite the confusing maze the castle has become.

52 A nobleman has hired an enchantress dressmaker to make a wonderful garment for his daughter and has asked the players to be bodyguards for the dressmaker when she arrives at the pier. The nobleman has heard rumors that the dressmaker is the target of an evil plot.

53 The players are mistaken for a troupe of actors who are meant to entertain the king *right now*. There is no saying no, and not being entertaining enough could lead to death...or worse.

54 A local shop has begun to sell a wide variety of small monsters as pets. Each creature is bound to a command crystal that keeps it tame and obedient. Soon, customers discover that the creatures become wild and mischievous should the crystal shatter.

55 A theater troupe who are friends of the players have lost their stage crew and they need the players to fill in. The players must shift scenes, raise and lower the curtain, and get props and lights in place. All while not being seen by the audience. The audience is loaded down with fruit and vegetables, ready to launch at any performer or stage crew who displeases them.

56 Several people have gone missing around the library. The librarian inside has been trapping them into a book and then recording how they deal with the loose ideas they have written. They hope observing these people will help them finish their novel.

57 A nobleman believes that a current play put on by a friendly theater troupe is a satire about him and his family. The players must stop the nobleman's plans and save the theater from the mercenaries hired to burn the theater down.

58 The lead actress of the touring theater group is trying to escape her controlling family. The troupe approaches the players to help smuggle the actress out of the theater during the play. However, the actress's family has guards attending this very performance to capture her and bring her back home.

59 The theater troupe won't go into their theater because the ghost light went out and they want to make sure no ghosts have taken up residence. Three ghosts have, and they don't want to leave and want to be included in all new productions.

60 The players come across a store with lavishly priced, extremely silly garments with appropriate magical enhancements. For example, a frog costume that enhances agility, a horse head mask that improves speed, a teddy bear suit that gives its wearer a devastating claw attack, and many others.

61 The theater troupe has a new play to premiere and is unaware that the scene before intermission is a ritual to summon real demons. Luckily, the players have free tickets to watch the show opening night.

62 A noble family accidentally left one child behind when they left the city for their winter home. The family has sent word back and the players have been hired to find the child, who is hiding somewhere in the mansion. The child has laid traps everywhere.

63 A wizard has come to the theater claiming that someone stole his cloak of disguises and demands to search the entire place and all of the actors.

THE THEATER OF BLOOD

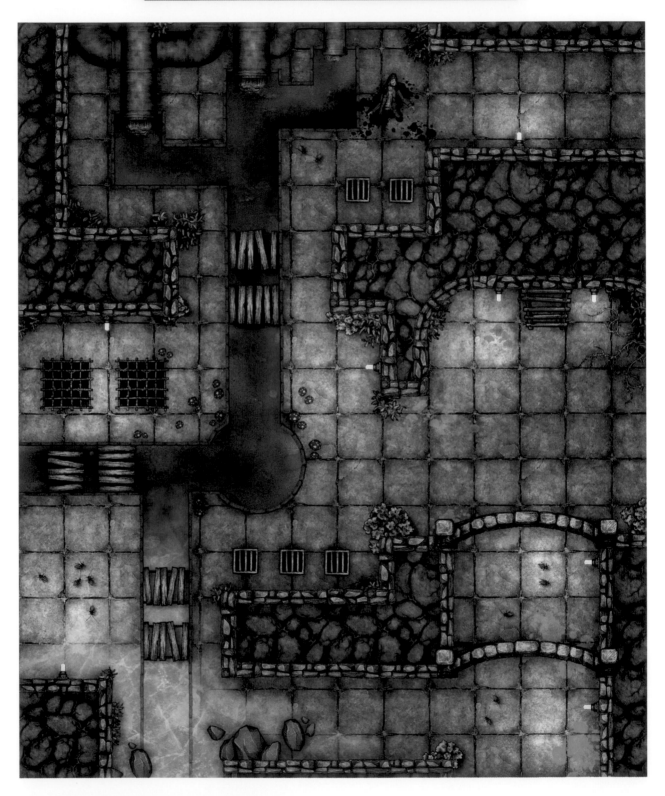

64 The city watch finds a half-eaten body where the sewers drain into the sea. They need extra help to see what may be living in the sewers underneath the city.

65 The city is celebrating Lucky Day. One day each year, the goddess of luck bestows the gift of incredible luck to all within the city limits. Some jump from buildings only to bounce back up unharmed. Others attempt to gamble (without much luck, as their fellow gamblers also have the luck charm). Still others prefer to leave the city entirely during this, as it tends to result in rampant chaos.

66 A druid has taken up residence in the sewers and is growing mushrooms. Local restaurants are thrilled by his product, but a wary merchant wants the players to follow the druid to make sure nothing evil is happening in the making of these mushrooms.

67 Thousands of bugs are pouring out of the sewer grates in the central square, attacking anyone and ruining all the food and merchandise. Strange music seems to be controlling the bugs. But who is playing the music?

68 A wizard approaches anyone who looks like they can cast spells and challenges them to a duel. It turns out there is a citywide wizard challenge going on with magical rankings. Whoever lands in the number one spot gets a fantastic item.

69 Strange moaning can be heard at night coming up from the sewers. All the merchants fear an undead outbreak and are looking to flee the area. However, it turns out to be a gang of thieves who wanted to scare the merchants into paying them to clear out the zombies.

70 The city's largest goalball game is happening today, and the people are in a fervor! Tickets to the event are all sold out. One wealthy individual, desperate to attend, says they will do anything for a ticket.

71 A street cleaner confides in secret that he was using an acidic slime creature to help clean and that he lost it down in the sewers. He's desperate to get his slime back.

72 The players have been invited to a royal wedding as special guests of the groom. A rival nation sees the gathering as the perfect time to kill the future monarchs and have planted assassins in the crowd. Good thing the players are there to protect the future king and queen!

73 A section of the street has mysteriously frosted over. Clearly something has gone wrong in the sewers below.

74 Today is election day in the city. The players learn through whispers that many in the city believe none of the votes are actually counted, and the current leader will never cede power.

75 In the sewers is a well-hidden, lively underground market where many undesirable things can be found. A local merchants guild will pay a pretty penny for the players to find and shut down this illegal competition.

76 Word has spread throughout the city of the players' deeds, and someone has put wanted signs up all over town with large bounties for the group. They are wanted dead or alive!

77 The players go to see a fortune teller. She recalls everything that has happened to the group thus far with uncanny accuracy, then makes a deeply disturbing prediction that is set to come true "on the next new moon, when the light has gone from the sky."

78 A noble approaches the players looking to pay to "go on an adventure!" It's obvious this noble will only slow you down, but if you can protect them for the duration, the pay is nice!

79 A body is found in the upstairs room of the tavern. There is no sign of how the man died, but the innkeeper states that the large snake tattoo on the man's arm is now gone.

80 Hidi Berrylaugh is a gnome hairstylist who uses magic to change people's hair in radical new ways. Her styles have become a sudden fad in the city and lines of people are showing up each day. She calls for the players to help her obtain more of the rare ingredient that fuels her magic.

81 The large tree at the center of the marketplace is dying and no one knows why. A local nobleman approaches the players to seek out the druid Vorin Silverleaf. She can help, but the locals have had a hard time reaching her home deep within a dangerous forest.

82 The city sheriff has hired the players to explore the poor area of town on rumors that a breakout of lycanthropy is running rampant through the area. A group of were-creatures has been uniting the poor and teaching them useful skills.

83 A baker flees her bakery shouting for everyone to get away. Shortly after her warning, the doors and windows bust out with masses of roiling dough pouring into the street. She confesses to the players that she stole a vial from a wizard thinking she knew how to use the substance in it.

84 Strange whining can be heard from an alleyway. Upon inspection, the players find a mastiff that has just given birth to five puppies.

85 On the last day of the harvest festival, a booming voice shouts, "At last, my revenge!" Then hundreds of squirrels pour into the marketplace and start attacking.

86 The party stumbles wearily into the room they've rented for the night. They had been told this wasn't the best inn in the city, but they weren't expecting the bed to attempt to consume whoever was unlucky enough to try sleeping on it.

87 A gnome wants to sell the city on a summoning circle transport system and hires the players to help them show proof of concept.

88 A gnome needs the players' help clearing out a number of buildings she just bought to make a woodland area within the city. But the noble who sold the buildings hid the fact that cult activity has been noted in that exact area.

89 The smells from this food cart are repulsive, but it has a large crowd of people happily eating the food.

90 A costume maker is way behind on orders for the upcoming festival and is hiring anyone to help out in any way they can. Payment is a costume of their choice.

91 An ancient dragon lands atop the castle and states, "At long last, I have come to claim what is rightfully mine!" No one knows what the dragon is referring to, but the old castle cook remembers seeing a tapestry that used to hang in the castle when she was a child. She vaguely remembers it depicted a scene with a dragon and a great knight.

92 An NPC the players have been trying to meet with recently has been making lots of excuses and has used the "my grandpa just died" excuse at least three times. If tracked down, they can see this person, covered in dirt, actually attending many funerals.

93 A weapon store clerk arrives one morning to a strange occurrence. The back wall seems to have exploded out, but all the bricks are suspended in air, slowly traveling away from the shop. More disturbingly, about a half-mile directly out from this explosion is a large monster similarly suspended, but gradually heading backward toward the shop.

94 The king is offering a large sum of gold to anyone who can make an ironclad defense plan for the towers at the gates to the kingdom. A horde of monsters is headed this way, but this tower will be the bottleneck they will have to go through.

95 The city is plagued with poltergeists and various undead annoyances. Most folks in the city treat this recent influx of ghosts as mostly a nuisance. They are willing to pay capable exterminators handsomely to rid them of the specters.

96 The mayor has been quietly paying off two local crime families but has run out of funds to keep doing so. She offers the players the last of her funds to help her get rid of one or both of the families.

97 The townsfolk have been seeing more cats around than usual. They seem to be mostly hanging around the castle. The players find that the young princess has been turning everyone into cats. They must find a way to stop the young royal without falling victim to her spell.

98 The parents of one of the characters invite the entire party to a ball. Over the course of the night, the player realizes their parents and all the guests have been replaced with nearly exact copies of themselves. They must find out what is really going on here before dawn...or else.

99 The players find themselves in an unfamiliar part of the city. They find shops and eateries unlike any they've seen in other parts of town. They explore everything this new street has to offer. After returning to other more familiar parts of the city, no one can remember the name of the street, and no townsfolk they ask are familiar with the shops they describe.

100 The players arrive in town just in time to see a procession of people marching down the main road. The leader of the procession greets the players and places a large jester hat on one of the characters. This character is now the Lord of Misrule. For the next three days, they must go around town playing pranks and having a generally raucous time, creating merriment for the townspeople.

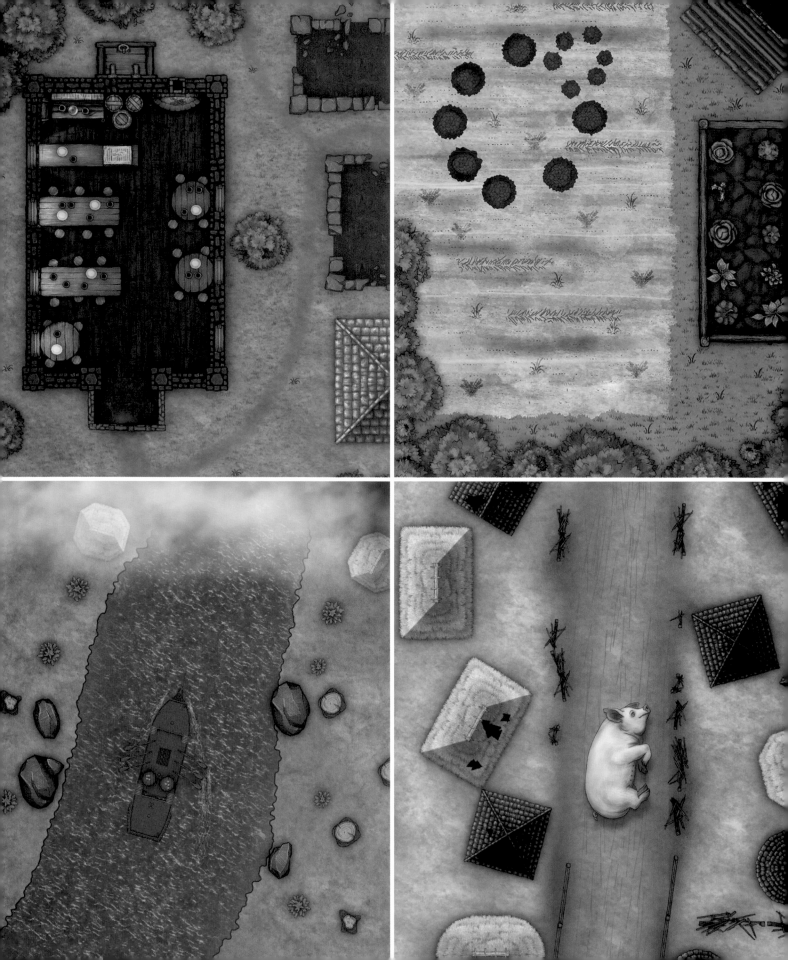

VILLAGE

Villages and towns provide some of the widest encounter variety of any location in an RPG. They're populous enough to support large social encounters, they're close enough to wilderness to easily explain the presence of just about any monster type, and they're contained enough to host stories about entire communities.

Often, villages are only temporary stopping points. The party stops at the nearest village to rest, has some encounter with the people there, and then heads back off on their main adventure.

Town encounters often involve doing someone a favor or performing a job, since there's almost always a shortage of skilled and equipped adventurers outside of the major cities. For the same reason, villages and towns are also places where the players' actions in encounters can have meaningful effects on the world.

By the same token, saving citizens from a monster attack in a village is a truly heroic act, while saving citizens from a monster attack in a city is just another Tuesday afternoon. With that in mind, think of ways in which your players can make a mark on these communities through the encounters. Then, a few story arcs later, bring the party back to a few of these spots to show how their actions are remembered by the townsfolk.

1. The players stumble upon a black market for necromancers who are selling illegally exhumed bodies for rituals.

2. A local folk hero, Freginald Jaygen, asks the players for help. Freginald doesn't want the kids in town to see that he has lost his fighting ability. He will pay the players to get rid of the monsters *and* make it look like he was the one to save the day.

3. A gnome in this snowy village hires the players to make as many snowballs as they can so she can test out her new invention—an automated ice cream maker. As she loads the machine up, it goes a bit haywire and starts shooting snowballs at everyone.

4. A figure in a lumpy white cloak is selling forever candles from a small storefront. When approached, they introduce themself as the Wodgian Wizard of the Wicks. Unfortunately, the new forever candles won't stop growing wax. Molten wax is spilling out of every cabinet in the store. If the players help, the wizard gives the players a card with the wizard's picture on it. This card can be used to cast a spell that refills any vessel with whatever was most recently inside it.

5. A villager has a terrible sickness. The village wizard thinks they can shrink the party down to microscopic size in order to do battle with the illness *inside* the person's body.

6. This village is led by a vile leader. The citizens live in fear. It seems like a change in leadership would really help the villagers.

7. The village tavern is a large and welcoming place, heavily decorated with antlers: antler wall hangings, sconces, even an antler chandelier. The burly tavern owner invites the players to join him on an elk hunt the next day. He wants to redecorate one of the upstairs rooms and needs more inspiration.

8. The townsfolk keep mentioning that it's Flat Thursday today. When questioned, they explain that the town is charged an exorbitant weekly tax by a giant who lives nearby. If the town can't pay, one of the villagers gets squished. Unfortunately, they're all out of money.

9. This village at the foot of a small mountain is covered in fresh snow. A local wizard is offering free teleports to the top for people who want to ski and sled for the day. A gang of marauders takes advantage of the distraction to attack the village.

10. The villagers have grown wary of an ever-increasing flock of crows. The crows have done nothing, but people are beginning to panic and want the birds killed. This is a test from a spirit to see how the town reacts. For every crow killed, a townsperson will also die.

11. A week ago a meteor struck near town. Since then, people have been slowly turning into plants. However, the meteor isn't the cause. It's just mischievous fairies in the nearby woods who have been playing tricks on the villagers.

12. This village has quarantined itself from the outside world. Most of the residents have some kind of disease that grows mushrooms on their faces. They warn you to stay far away, but also implore you to help them.

13 All the citizens here worship a god none of the players have heard of. Their devotion is complete and obsessive. Anyone seen contradicting the very strange customs of this god is put to trial.

14 In this village is a remote training school for warriors. Sadly, the headmaster just passed away and the players get wrapped up in the dispute over who will lead the school next.

15 When the players arrive to the village at night, the whole place is empty. But at dawn, all the townsfolk are suddenly there...only to disappear again when night falls. The villagers don't believe the players when confronted about the strange disappearances.

16 The well at the center of town has gone dry. When the party investigates, they find a door at the bottom of the well that has been shut. Opening the door, they find it opens to another well at the bottom of a faraway lake. But who closed the door, and why?

17 A sudden snowfall has dropped over 3 feet of snow on the village, trapping people in their homes. The citizens enlist the players' help, as there is a superstition that a sudden snowfall like this is a portent that abominable snowmen will attack.

18 This village hosts a festival around a flower that blooms only once a year and only for a day.

19 Music, signs, and brightly colored streamers indicate that today is some sort of party, but all the townsfolk look melancholy. The players learn that at midnight, several children from the village will be randomly assigned as sacrifices to the "god king" that rules here.

20 A nearby sorcerer has cursed the town to always be under clouds and rain. The townsfolk are miserable and want the players to find some way to deal with the problem.

21 A band of goblins has taken up residence in the nearby hills. The town wants them gone but the goblins only want to trade in peace.

22 A passing salesperson sold a local farmer a miracle growth formula. Now the plants are threatening to take over the whole town, and most of the villagers are trapped in the constricting vines.

23 A family of nobles have been forced from their homes and have taken up residence in this simple village. The villagers hate their constant demands and insults. The noble family will be attacked unless some sort of peace can be found.

24 The city is celebrating Victory over Gruthorryn Day, a local celebration of victory over a dragon that once ruled this area with malice and cruelty. The celebration means free food, drink, and a generally happy vibe from everyone in the city.

25 Most of the townsfolk here talk in a strange, robotic manner. The mayor is jovial, but dismissive of any questions about the town. An investigation could reveal that the mayor is systematically replacing the people in town with his ever-expanding collection of changelings.

26 The annual fair is happening! There are magical Ferris wheel rides, delicious treats, and a funhouse where several villagers went in...but never came out.

27 While staying in the inn of this small village, a portal opens up and three stern-looking elves step out. They demand to see the mayor, stating simply that the contract is due.

 28 This town has a tavern that is completely run by intelligent dogs. The food is terrible, but it seems quite safe.

29 The tavern has a sign calling for adventurers to collect a list of very rare and difficult-to-obtain ingredients. The reward is a nice stack of gold and the promise of being able to "try the dish I'm making!"

30 The town is having a strange mock funeral for the oldest person in town. It's a joyous but odd celebration. Secretly, the person wants to die but has been cursed with immortality.

31 A poster advertising the tavern's talent show is tonight! And look at that, the prize for first place is something the players have been longing for!

32 A hopeful young person sits at a small table with pamphlets promising fame and fortune. They explain that they are offering payment for mapping the "here there be dragons" part of the nearby ocean.

33 The new tavern owner found a locked door in the basement that only the previous and long-dead owner knew how to open. If anyone can open the door, the new owner promises a generous reward—depending on what is behind that door.

34 A bard sings hilarious songs that are way too close to the players' adventures to be coincidence. When confronted, the bard swears she doesn't know them and has never seen them before.

 35 An explorer in the tavern has a proposition: If the players fund her, she will share a percentage of her discoveries with them. She will return to the tavern in 1d6 days with a precious gem. If they continue to finance her, have her run into the players occasionally with unusual items.

36 It's the annual guess-the-brew contest. A dwarven ale master has made an ale that has twenty-one flavors in it. If anyone can guess all twenty-one, he will give them his ever-filling ale stein to use for the next year.

37 A local innkeeper is trying to sell his inn to a semi-famous hero and needs the players to help put on a good show to make the sale.

38 It's time for the harvest festival! There's an open-air market spanning the entire village filled with vendors, fortune tellers, bootleggers, and carnival games. Perhaps the players spring to action when a necromancer attacks the festival with an army of skeletons, or perhaps that doesn't happen, and they just enjoy the festival.

39 The patrons of this tavern are looking at the players warily. When prodded, the barkeep will point out the bounty illustration of figures looking remarkably like the players.

40 The leader of this village is a pastor promising "visions of the true god" to the village's population. In truth, the pastor is running a drug ring and the denizens of this village are the unlucky, highly addicted customers.

41 The players arrive in town but don't know that the inhabitants are an invading force. The real villagers are tied up in the basement of the tavern. The tavern owner is the only real villager left and is desperate for the players' help.

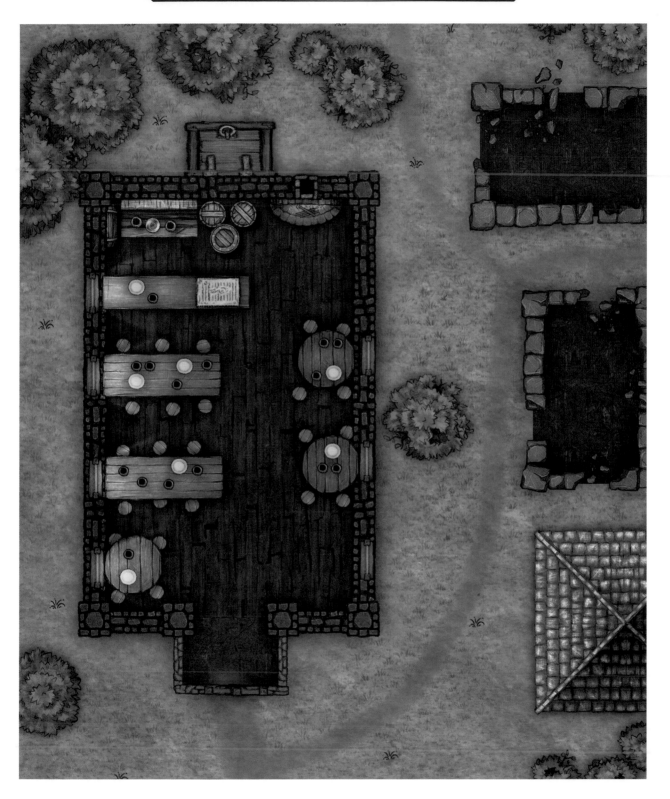

42 One farmer's pumpkin has grown to an enormous size—nearly as tall as their home. Yesterday, the farmer could hear scratching noises inside the pumpkin.

43 Children have been wandering into a wheat field and not returning. Upon inspection, there is a large circle of runes dug into the ground that seems to be a portal to somewhere.

44 A farmer is upset that a strange half-bird, half-bear creature has taken over his barn, and he wants it gone. The creature, however, has a newborn cub and will fiercely attack anyone who approaches.

45 This village is filthy. Apparently, some time ago, the garbage collection and disposal workers went on strike and never got their demands met. Now the town just lives in their own mess.

46 The local farmers need to expand their fields and need help clearing the nearby woods. However, the denizens of the woods aren't willing to give up their homes without a fight.

47 This village has many dungeoneering shops. Each shopkeeper name-drops the local dungeon, and there's lots of signage that "warns" of this dangerous dungeon but is clearly designed to get adventurers to go. The villagers and the dungeon denizens here run a kind of adventurer tourist industry with no real danger, or valuable loot.

48 The farmer claims he found his son in a giant pumpkin, but the town thinks he kidnapped a nearby lord's child. The farmer is telling the truth and the child is from another world.

49 A farmer is convinced his cows are being replaced by things that look exactly like his cows, but he swears they aren't his cows. If the players choose to investigate, they will find that the farmer is actually right. The cows are shape-shifters spying on the countryside.

50 A group of centaurs is on the run from the local authorities and are hiding in a nearby farm. They beg the players to help them, claiming they have been falsely accused of stealing from the king. If investigated further, the players find that the centaurs actually did commit the crime.

51 A strange object fell from the sky and landed in the middle of some farmland. Now all the root vegetables have come to life and are attacking the farmer and the village.

52 A farmer is begging for help to get back his prize cow that was poached and points the group in the direction he thinks it went. He's neglecting to mention that a gigantic bird took his cow, hoping the players will just kill the bird without question.

53 A gnome's harvesting machine is out of control and he needs help trying to shut it down. He really doesn't want it destroyed.

54 A farmer discovers all the vegetables she planted have sprouted gold pieces. She needs help gathering them all in as quickly as possible. If the players choose to help her, they only have a few hours before the powerful gremlin that cast the spell comes to collect the gold himself.

55 The riverboat captain has been telling stories of the next stop for days. He speaks highly of this village's food and people. His mood darkens when black smoke is seen on the horizon. The village has been attacked, and the captain urges the players to investigate. Fire demons are spilling from a summoning circle in the village center.

56 A dream-monster torments the nights of all this village's inhabitants. Through meditation and lucid dream training, the players can gain the ability to go into these dreams as much more experienced and powerful versions of themselves.

57 A thick fog forces the riverboat to stop at an abandoned-looking village. The captain tells the players the village is cursed. If the players investigate, they find a bunch of friendly people who don't understand why no one stops in their village. What is really going on here?

58 Two rival gangs have been fighting over the land here for years now, and this town has a giant line painted through it and through the middle of the only inn in town. There are two separate entrances, and tension hangs in the air everywhere.

59 A band of riverboat pirates can be seen attacking the town up ahead. Shouts and screams can be heard long before the village comes into view. The pirates are taking anything and anyone they want aboard their ship.

60 A shaded corner of this village has a building with a large eye painted on it. Inside, a psychic offers to tell the players' fortunes for a price. The psychic reveals two truths and a lie to any player who pays the fee.

61 A team of young investigators and their loyal hound are definitely going to get themselves killed investigating the extremely haunted local decrepit manor house. The players can choose to bodyguard them for a meager reward and the satisfaction of saving some meddling kids.

62 This riverside village is small but rich, as it is a major stop on the trade route. A local wizard set up a casino on a riverboat that is actually where most of the town's money is made. The games are magically rigged to make sure everyone loses eventually.

63 Through a misunderstanding, the players are thrown in the surprisingly secure village jail. There is already someone in the cell. As the day goes on and it becomes clear the villagers will not be releasing them, the cellmate warns that he is a werewolf and tonight is a full moon.

64 This town has strange strings decorating most surfaces. In the day, it looks a little messy, but as soon as the sun sets, the strings light up with bright, glowing colors. The church here is the most densely decorated and appears to be dedicated to a "neon god."

65 The players have been warned that the next village on the river trade route is a bit unusual but harmless. Everyone in the village is a humanoid frog and they make excellent pottery; they are quite friendly if a bit unusual.

66 This village is plague-ridden. The illness is airborne and leaves the sick with an aversion to light and an iron deficiency. At first glance, it may appear that the village is overrun with vampires.

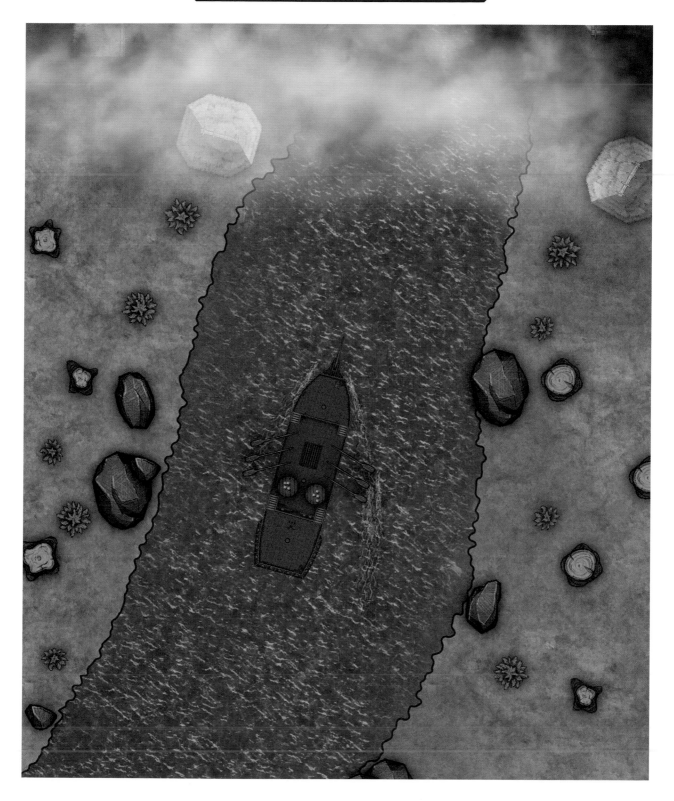

67 This village is strange. Signage has obvious misspellings, buildings are improperly constructed, and other odd blunders abound. If investigated, the players uncover that the mayor of this town was previously the "village idiot," who found a magical artifact and now rules over their previous detractors.

68 A giant pig has fallen asleep in the center of the village and the farmer can't get the pig to move in any way. A crafty party member might notice there is more to this massive pig than meets the eye....

69 Signs around this village proclaim "No trespassing," "Turn away now OR ELSE," and further, more ominous warnings. If the players proceed, the entire village sets upon the intruders. They seem to act in concert, as if they are all linked, acting with one consciousness.

70 The village dollmaker's creations have all come to life and are terrorizing the village. The dolls attack as if they were their real-life counterparts.

71 The players must break into the home of an obviously evil lord of the village. Maybe it's to steal his riches, maybe it's to rescue some of the folks that have gone missing, or maybe it's for revenge. Either way, this lord has got to go.

72 The largest building in the village is the lumber mill. Recently, all production stopped when all the tools came to life and began attacking workers. An observant player will notice one of the most recently cut trees in the forest looks like it could have been home to a wood sprite.

73 The villagers here have been hiding deserters of a war that is raging in a kingdom to the south. A very persuasive character can find out that they are deserters from the invading army who think the war is unjust. If the players stay in town, they will encounter soldiers looking for these deserters.

74 The villagers here tell of an ancient blessing that allows the dead to come back to life as long as they stay within the village. If the players wish to watch a final death, in two days a villager is being walked to the graveyard far outside of town where they will willingly be dead forever.

75 After the townsfolk see one of the players perform magic, a mob of pitchfork-wielding farmhands forms to chase the "demons" out of town.

76 This town only has children; there are no adults around. The children swear they don't know where the adults are, and by the looks of it, they are doing fine without them.

77 This village is way off the beaten path. You were led here, but you can't remember by whom. Everyone here is very kind, but it becomes clear the villagers have enchanted the surrounding woods to capture travelers and will try to keep them here by any means.

78 While walking around this village, the very perceptive will notice that sometimes the ground sounds hollow. The town is rumored to have been built on top of an older town. The old town was said to be guarding a vast treasure, and the people here have been trying to search and dig up the old town to find the riches.

79　The mayor of this small town is thrilled when the players arrive. He begs the players to set up a vocational course to teach the young adults of the town skills to defend their village. He promises they will be well paid for their efforts.

80　All of the farmer's sheep have somehow been attached together, making the whole flock one giant moving mass of wool. She desperately needs to shear the sheep so that they can be separated again. If the players help, she offers some of the magically sticky wool as a reward.

81　A farmer is trying to sell the party his flock of riding birds. He shows the party how they can ride these massive, ostrich-looking creatures. He's even selling them at a discount, as the party would be free advertising around the nation.

82　A young girl approaches the party asking for help. The girl claims that her pet goat has been talking to her and promising her fine dresses and jewels if she will just kiss the goat once. Magical inspection shows that a spell has been placed on the goat allowing a caster to talk through the goat.

83　This village is completely made up of gnomes. Every aspect of life is run by magic. The gnomes don't want money to stay here, but they do ask if the party can give up some magic to help keep things going smoothly. One or two spells per person is enough.

84　There are no fires allowed in this village. The townsfolk say that any fires attract the beast, and let the players stay if they promise to not use any fire. If the players do, a 50-foot bear stomps toward the village screaming about preventing fires.

85　A player has been accused of stealing a sacred weapon. When the players ask for proof, the real weapon is found to still be in the owner's vault. The player has a replica... from which an evil shadow now emerges and attempts to steal the real weapon.

86　The players enter this village to shouts of "The hero has returned!" They are surrounded by happy villagers and swept to the center of town where a statue in the exact likeness of one of the characters stands. Everyone is eager to hear the story of how the hero procured the stolen money they were sent to reclaim.

87　A figure shrouded in a dark cloak walks into town carrying a writhing sack, saying they "took care of it." They demand payment. When the town refuses, the figure casts a spell on everyone in town (including the party), shrinking them all. They then upend the sack, spilling out the rats they caught.

88　Two small gingerbread people run out of the small bakery and flee the town. A look inside the bakery reveals a young boy covered in flour and holding a wand. He's cackling with glee, shouting, "Be free!" as he brings various cookie people to life.

89　Everyone here has a cat that shadows them at all times. Any attempt to interfere with a cat and villager will provoke a fight. The locals worship a cat god who has blessed them with these familiars.

90　The people of this village are living under constant threat from a strange woman living in a high tower at the far end of town. If pressed, a villager will reveal the woman is a siren and they have to keep her happy so that she doesn't sing and drive them all mad.

91 A local farmer cast a spell he didn't fully understand. It went wrong, and now eight-legged goats are running all around the town, eating everything and spitting out webs at anyone who bothers them.

92 The local village has put out fliers for anyone to help. The river they use every day for water seems to be making everyone sick and they don't know why. Anyone who goes way upstream can find a large mining facility that is pouring some sort of foul substance into the river.

93 A local priest has stumbled upon the truth that the mayor of this village is a dragon in disguise who has been hoarding the villagers' taxes and leaving the town in disrepair. The mayor wants to eliminate the threat. Who do the players decide to help?

94 This village is seemingly abandoned, but upon further inspection every home has villagers busily writing in large books. Someone explains these people document the events of the whole world in giant books that eventually ascend to the library of the god of knowledge.

95 This village is overrun by 10-foot-tall chickens who often mistake the villagers for tasty food. The villagers will give the players free lodging and a nice reward if they can slay all of these monster chickens.

96 The whole village square and most of the road is covered in rabbits. If the rabbits are struck, they duplicate. If two rabbits that exactly match are placed together in a quiet place, they merge back into one rabbit.

97 The players approach a large barn where an elf asks them for help with some research. There are two rooms in the barn; the players can choose which inhabitants to fight. In the first room is one duck the size of a black bear. In the second room are ten black bears, each the size of a duck. The elf will pay handsomely for this research.

98 It's the thimble festival in this village. Through the year, local farmers have been trying to grow tiny prize-winning crops. All these bonsai vegetables are on display and the day ends with a mini-pie eating contest. One farmer accuses another of using shrinking magic on his vegetables, and the whole festival will be ruined unless the players can ascertain that no magic was involved.

99 This village spends a week harvesting clouds to store water for the upcoming dry months. They go up in large air balloons and use special nets to capture the clouds. This year there are many dark cloud banks, which the villagers say house sky giants who must not be disturbed or they will cause trouble.

100 This town consists of only two buildings: a simple plain tavern and a lavish manor. The innkeeper tells the party that they are on the grounds of the famous enchantress Violet Magnolia. Next week, people will flock to the town for the Magnolia fashion show, where people will put on their most eye-catching and outrageous fashions in order to be chosen to have one item enchanted to their liking. Anyone can join for a fee.

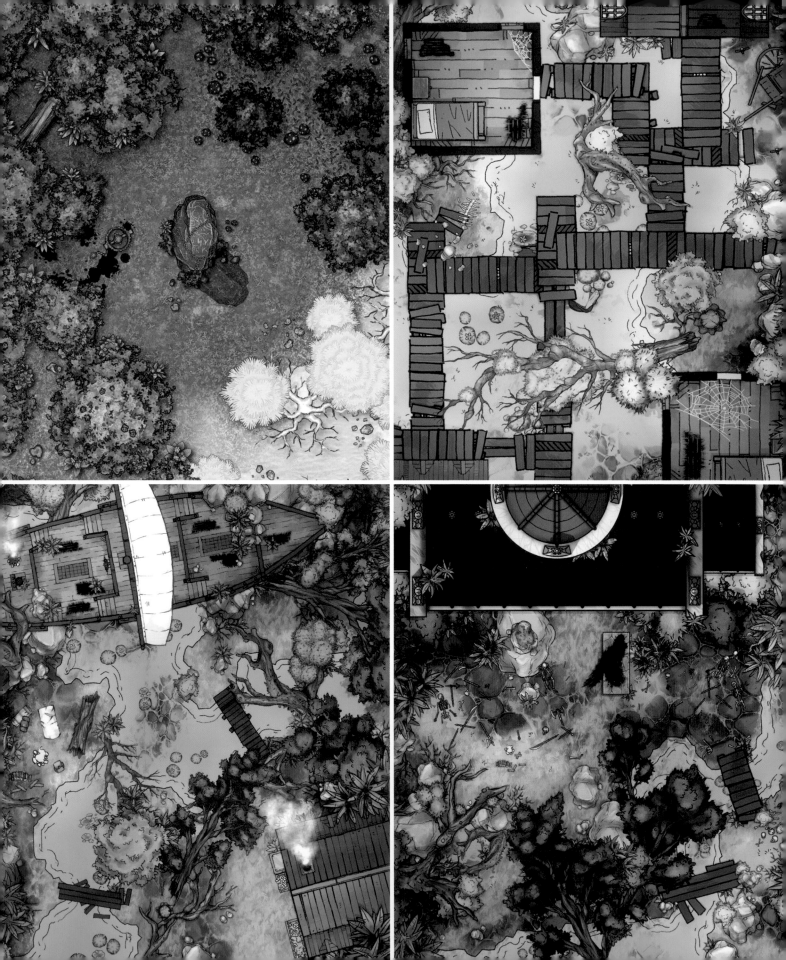

FOREST/SWAMP

The swamp and forest take you deep into the wild. No matter how suited up you are with magical doodads, when you're deep in a muddy woods you're bound to feel out of your depth. The swamp and forest are perfect spots to create that effect, so this table of encounters is designed to work in either location. This far from civilization, you've got to keep your wits about you!

It's not all harrowing tales of survival though. Dangerous, sure, but both the swamp and the forest are teeming with life. Fights are likely to be ambushes from beautiful, deadly creatures—unless the players are hunting a quarry of their own!

1   A loud buzzing leads the players to a giant beehive built high in the air between three trees. Giant bees swarm in and out. Could this be the source of the fabled honey that can cure any wound or disease with just one taste?

2   A group of swamp people is tracking down a boar that killed their leader, Filthy Jyn. However, a wizard actually switched the boar's and Jyn's souls. She is trying to convince the party of her true identity before her clan kills the boar she resides in.

3   A barely noticeable ladder is carved into the side of a large tree, leading up to a massive treehouse with some clearly valuable items inside. Unfortunately, some nasty-looking, very large birds have taken the house as their nest.

4   A forlorn human is standing guard over a crystal coffin in the middle of the woods and begs for help to free their loved one from an evil spell.

5   The players are put into a trance by the toxic fumes of a strange plant near their path. One of them is now working against the others. Randomly select a player. Secretly communicate to that player that they are now playing as a pod person disguised as their character. Their goal is to convince others to go into the sinister cabin at the far end of the path.

6   A weird snow suddenly fills this part of the forest and seems to be coming out from a hole under a large rock farther in. Inside, an ice creature is being held against its will.

7   Deep in the forest is a castle made entirely out of rose bushes. Beautiful blooms are everywhere. The elvish inhabitants are barely tolerant of anyone who isn't druidic in some way.

8   Hordes of biting, stinging bugs have been eating the players alive. A wandering merchant in strange clothing with an even stranger face offers a salve to ward off the insects for a payment "to be collected later."

9   This tall, thick tree is mostly hollow inside. Moving in and out of various holes within the trunk are tiny fairy dragons who use this tree as their home. They are curious but harmless and can be befriended with a bit of food and gold to follow a player as a companion.

10 The players see an impressive-looking gorilla off in the distance watching them. If the players move too close and seem at all aggressive, the gorilla will attack.

11 The players come across a cluster of skeletons surrounding a large tower. A strange old necromancer lives inside and wishes to find the key to bring back his now dead adventuring party.

12 A large tree stands alone in this clearing. The area beneath the tree looks like the night sky complete with stars. Anyone standing under the tree no longer sees the tree but, instead, a strange night sky.

13 A mossy tree introduces themself as the Wodgian Wizard of the Weald. Unfortunately, their moss-growing experiments have ensnared them entirely. They'd like freedom, but can't bear for any moss to die in the process. If the players help, the wizard offers a card with their picture on it. This spell card can make a plant grow gigantic.

14 A young forest spirit captures the players, shrinks them down, and pits them against stag beetles and other small creatures (that are now gargantuan to the players) in gladiatorial combat.

15 The players stumble into a coliseum made of trees and vines. This is the site of the annual Secret Magicks Athletic Tournament. Events like the no-fly long jump, the wand vault, and the angry mile are featured. Anyone who thinks their magic is up to the standards of the competition may enter!

16 The players are caught in a maddening forest maze. They are sure they've passed this same red-flowering bush before. Mist is beginning to get denser on the forest floor as the sun sets.

17 High in the trees is a large city that protects this part of the forest. As the players pass, elves and humans drop from the trees and demand that they pay the toll to move through this part of the forest.

18 While traveling near a swamp, the players find a strange bit of nearly transparent parchment. Further inspection finds another, much longer piece. It's 100 feet long...and clearly shed from a snake. Just behind them, something large is moving in the swamp water.

19 The players are hired to hunt down a hag in the swamp who has been eating children. The woman is actually a powerful wizard who has been taking care of lost or abandoned children. She will only let the children go if the players promise to help the children.

20 A sudden earthquake shakes everything around the players. After the quake dies down, large bubbles float out of the swamp and explode, spraying poisonous gas everywhere.

21 Beautiful singing can be heard from a tower deep in the woods. It has no doors and only one window at the top. If the players make any noise, a mass of long hair falls out of the window and attempts to entangle them.

22 A young lady asks for help finding her love who was to meet her in the woods. Eventually, the players will lose sight of her and a young man will approach asking for the same help.

23 A hut walking on chicken legs is quickly approaching the players. The woman in the hut yells that the players' smell offends her, and she offers her hut to quickly get them out of the forest and away from her.

24 This part of the woods is dying from rot and decay, including the animated trees that live in this area. The rot has robbed them of their will, and they lash out at anyone who gets too close.

25 According to legend, there is a tree made out of pure gold in the center of the forest. Unfortunately, anyone who can find it is turned into gold if they touch it.

26 A group of actors is performing a historical play in a clearing in the woods. If the players interrupt the show, they will be attacked by the invisible audience watching the show. If they stay and watch the play, they gain valuable insight into the events happening around them.

27 A group of satyrs comes across the players and offers them wine and fruit. They are loud, hilarious, and clearly having a great time. They urge the players to join. If they agree, they have an amazing time but also lose five days as they lose all track of time.

28 The trees in this clearing look like the bark is crawling. The movement is from the hundreds of butterflies that are beating their wings in unison. If disturbed, the butterflies will swarm around the feet of the players and attempt to open a portal that will send them far away.

29 The players spy a large frog staring at them from the bushes. If approached, it looks worried, then two *much* larger frogs appear from the surrounding foliage. They scoop up the smaller frog and beg you not to mention you saw them. They are a rare species trying to remain hidden.

30 Around the base of these trees are extraordinarily large truffles. One of these would fetch an impressive price in any major city even if it is taken there in pieces. The giant boar that lives here isn't happy to find anyone messing with its food supply and attacks accordingly.

31 The players stumble across a group of gnomes using a series of wires to quickly travel through the forest. If asked nicely, the gnomes will allow the players to travel for a small fee.

32 In a clearing, there is a large standing stone. While the players investigate, writing appears on the stone with a meeting place and a time. If the players wait around, they will see a person approach, read the note, and then write on the stone themself. Mysterious...

33 There is some sort of competition happening in this clearing. It has been divided into four parts, with each section representing a season. Each season has a champion to fight for the grand prize. One of the seasons wants the players to fight in place of their champion; if they win, the players take the prize.

34 The players encounter a glade of fairies who want to play a game. Any game will do! If the players win, the fairies will do their best to grant the players a wish. If the fairies win, the players must do all the fae chores.

35 A wounded deer is trapped in a snare and surrounded by vicious beasts. If the players save the deer, it's revealed to be a grateful druid who had transformed at the wrong moment.

36 In the middle of a clearing is a large, faintly glowing stone with a rusted chain wrapped around it. It looks like there was something written on the stone, but the weather has made it difficult to read.

37 The group collectively gets caught in several different traps set out to catch large game, not people...they hope!

38 In the center of this clearing is a large rock that seems to be covering an old well. The faint outline of a house can be seen a few feet away from this well. There are scratching noises from something beneath the rock.

39 A wounded druid approaches the players in desperate need of help. Poachers are hunting in his sanctuary and he needs them stopped.

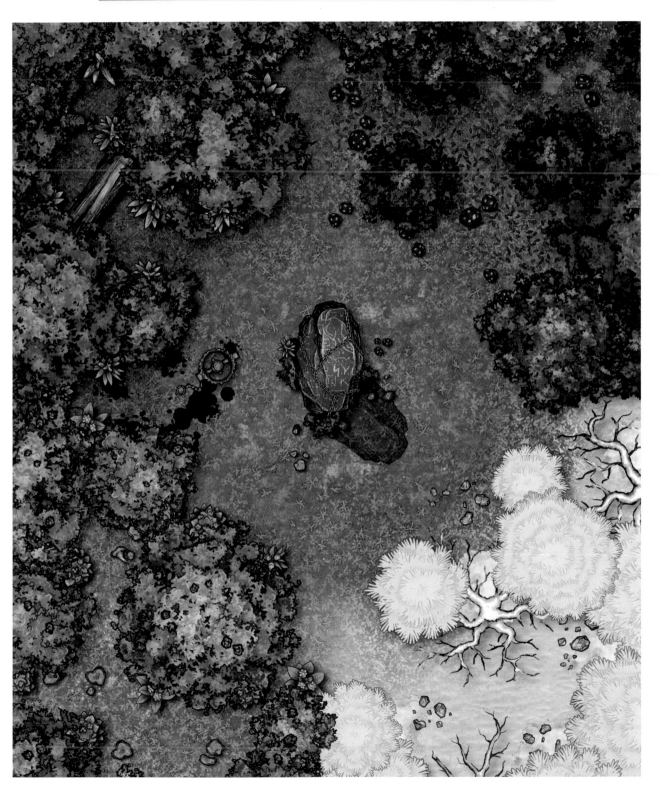

40 A strange fog covers everything here, making traveling in the swamp extra dangerous. In the fog, will-o'-the-wisps try to light the correct path, but the players may find the eerie lights to be unsettling.

41 An old crone approaches you asking for food. If the players refuse to help, the crone curses the group. They are now, collectively, the Swamp Guardian. They must defend the swamp from any who would endanger it. The only way out is to find another soul dedicated to protecting the swamp.

42 At the center of the swamp is a large dark crystal with what looks to be a person inside. Locals say that the swamp appeared only two years ago. Could this be the cause?

43 The players come upon an abandoned village sticking out in the middle of the swamp. However, mud people are living here and don't take kindly to anyone exploring their homes.

44 The players come upon a witch coven ecstatic to see them. The witches offer a warm, delicious meal. The following morning, as everyone is nursing magical hangovers, the coven offers the adventurers ongoing work finding ingredients for their incantations.

45 In a strange abandoned village in the swamp, weird lights can be seen at night hovering in the windows. The will-o'-the-wisps take a keen interest in anyone new to their home.

46 Bog stench has gotten so strong it's at risk of incapacitating the players if they don't do something about this olfactory obstacle.

47 Folks say that the village just appeared in the middle of the swamp one day. A coven of hags lurks within the village, hoping to capture and eat anyone who comes to explore.

48 An alligator charges out of the muck and attempts to pull the player in the back into the murky swamp.

49 A band of strange humanoid monsters quickly sets upon the players atop their swamp boats and attempts to catch the group in their nets for their next meal.

50 The splash from a giant tail covers the players in swamp water. Looking up, they see a giant beaver, clearly protecting its den, getting ready to slap its massive tail once again and swat the party away.

51 Within a large gathering of pine trees is a simple-looking shrine. In front of the shrine are the rinds and cores of many exotic fruits in a small basket. Anyone who offers up a piece of fruit gains the blessing of the forest.

52 Any player who has been walking in the swamp water will have one to fifty leeches under their clothing trying to drain them of blood.

53 One day, the bell in the tower of an abandoned village in the swamp began to chime. The humanoid frog creatures that now live in this village have been using the bell to call their exploration teams back home.

54 A large bear is charging toward the players when a giant hand grabs it. The trees bend to reveal a large giant chewing up the bear and eyeing the players next.

55 A swamp dwelling seems like an enticing rest stop. Once inside, everyone hears music. This tune forces all the players to dance *hard*. They keep bashing wildly into each other.

56 A run-down ship is half sunk in the swamp mud, but clearly someone lives there. It's an old witch who can tell anyone's fortune...if they are willing to pay the price.

57 An imp sitting by a fire says they will answer any question truthfully if the players can guess their name. The imp's name is written in demonic on the back of their shirt. If anyone can read that, the imp is very interested in them and will show up from time to time going forward.

58 A rogue lightning bolt from a careless wizard has sparked a fire. A nearby elven tree village is dangerously close to the flames.

59 A flock of griffins flies overhead, majestically heading toward their nests. A group of poachers approaches the players. They can either join in the hunt to capture the lucrative creatures or attempt to stop the poachers.

60 The forest spirits like to play pranks on anyone who spends the night in the woods: hiding weapons, taking food, etc. The spirits require a favor for them to leave you alone.

61 Ivy grows all over the trees in this section of the woods. It fills the canopy, blocking out most of the sun. As the players move through the area, the ivy shifts and coalesces into a dragon made of ivy demanding to see what treasures they bring.

62 A door stands alone in the middle of a clearing with a sign that says simply "Dusk on the 6th day." At that time, the door connects to a tavern full of creatures and people from around the world. The host at the door welcomes them and states no fighting is allowed within the Moonside Tavern.

63 A large wolf pack has caught the players' scent and has been tracking them through the woods. The pack attempts to isolate the last person in line and attack.

64 An explorer famed for her dramatic disappearance is actually alive and well, living on her own in the wilds. Her weariness for others means she's quick to defend her cabin by force.

65 This opulent tavern feels out of place but is a much-needed break. The welcoming hosts are eager to feed their new arrivals as much as they can eat. However, this is all an illusion. The hosts are actually human-spider hybrids who want to fatten up their guests before devouring them.

66 Skeletons half stuck in the mud around the edges of this village hint at the trouble waiting inside. Swamp trolls lurk within the abandoned buildings. They have placed an empty treasure chest here, hoping to lure in unsuspecting adventurers.

67 In a cabin deep in the woods, there's a man who's pleasant, but hiding something. If the players can get him away from the cabin, he will reveal the house is forcing him to lure travelers in so it can trap them in the basement and devour them. If the players eat any of the food, they will fall asleep.

68 This odd citadel seems out of place in the twisted landscape of the swamp. Even the gnarled dead trees don't seem to be willing to approach this dark building. There only seems to be one door in front of which sits a large slab with dried bloodstains over its surface. Carved into the slab are these words: "To enter here, you must make an appropriate sacrifice." Only when a humanoid is killed on the slab will the doors open to the citadel and its secrets.

69 A forlorn-looking woman slouches through the swamp with her back to the players. If anyone calls out to her, she turns, revealing a hideous visage. Anyone not wise enough to turn away quickly is cursed with bad luck. If the players attack her, she is a vicious fighter. Her death doesn't end the curse.

70 Deep in the swamp, an impressive citadel juts out of the mud. Hissing can be heard all around as humanoid snake people attack the players in an attempt to capture them. They plan to sacrifice the players to their massive snake god that slithers around the swamp.

71 The players spot a three-headed bear eating some honey. One of the heads is busy eating while the other two are scanning the forest for the next meal. Suddenly, one of the heads sniffs the air, and all three heads turn to face the players.

72 This strange swamp citadel seems to be the last refuge for the hopeless who have been driven out of their homes. The people here keep an uneasy peace and are barely surviving on the meager offerings in the swamp. The denizens of the citadel will try to beg for help from strong, well-rested players but will attack weary or weak ones.

73 It's clear that no one has been to this citadel in ages. The weapons are rusted and look ancient. The main door to the interior of the citadel is held shut by magic that is beginning to fail. Inside is a tomb that holds an ancient vampire eager to be set free. If the players break the seal, a starving vampire will leap free. Otherwise, the players can try to recreate the magic to reseal the citadel.

74 A strange-looking book floats slightly on the mud. Anyone with magical talent can attempt to decipher the strange spells within the book. Those who take time reading and working with the book will eventually hear a voice asking them if they want to form a pact with the power of the book to learn all of its secrets.

75 Sitting next to a pool of water is an ancient elf who looks at the group with eyes thick with cataracts, motioning for them to sit and talk for a while. If they do, the elf points to the pool where one person will be able to see a clear vision of their future. If they are hostile, the elf will frown and a water elemental will attack.

76 Music can be heard in the distance, but it's oddly paced—as if the player isn't really into it. At the source of the music, there is clearly a forest "celebration" going on, but no one here seems happy. Everyone is melancholy, joylessly going through the motions of dancing, eating, etc.

77 A group of wild-looking gnomes bursts from the trees riding on velociraptors. They surround the players, accusing them of scaring away their prey. They demand help in tracking the beast, which is a large burrowing monster with thick armor plates.

78 A giant, white grizzly bear sits outside a large den. She is surrounded by smaller bears of all types. She approaches the players and smells the air around them. If they have killed any bears in this forest she will attack. If they haven't, she will ask that they leave her woods, offering a bear escort to see them safely out.

79 There is a henge in this clearing made from petrified wood. A rune-carved bird-bath in the center is seemingly filled with the stars themselves. Spending time studying here will reveal that these star patterns match ones in the sky. The runes can be manipulated to send the players to far-off locations.

80 A large, pulsating sack is bound to the canopy above. If prodded, the sack explodes into hundreds of baby spiders (though still large). The infant spiders view whoever disturbed the sack as their mother. They will follow, attempt to hang on to, and protect their "mommy."

81 The players meet a strange little man trying to pull his bag out of the swamp. He asks for help getting his surprisingly heavy bag out of the muck. With the players occupied, he motions for his tiny skeleton familiar to steal anything that looks magical. If the players attack the man, he will fight until he can steal something and disappear, or he takes too much damage and disappears.

82 A group of bandits waits along the road to ambush anyone who passes through their forest. If spoken to, they say they are nobles run off from their ancestral lands. They offer to pay the players to help them take back their birthright.

83 A 2-foot-diameter circle of mushrooms on the ground seems ominous. If anything goes inside, it is transported to a beautiful village just below the forest floor. The forest dwarves all have mushrooms growing on them. They offer unique items for purchase and a very strange bed-and-breakfast if the players need to rest.

84 One of the players is hit on the head by an acorn. Looking up, they are surprised to see hundreds of squirrels with strange glowing eyes. When they have exhausted their projectiles, the squirrels leap to attack.

85 Some children have built treehouses here as a "secret base," but it seems like they are living here. Talking to the kids reveals their parents "got caught by the night-time vine" and that's why they stay above the forest floor as much as possible.

86 Shadows in this clearing are closing in upon a wounded and dying unicorn. The unicorn begs for help, promising if they are healed fully, they can drive away the shadows.

87 A strange, unsettling cloaked figure sits on a stump beneath a tangle of trees. A pair of peculiar eyes peer out from beneath the hood. It will answer any yes or no question truthfully by nodding or shaking its head. If the players touch the cloak, it bursts into leaves, fluttering to the ground in a pile.

88 A low mist rolls in out of nowhere and obscures the path. Slowly the fog gets heavier with wisps of mist easily reaching waist-high on a human. Low to the ground where the fog is densest, it is acidic and will eat through anything left in it for too long.

89 A fox runs past the players and winks at them. Off in the distance, the braying of hounds can be heard with sounds of people moving quickly through the brush. Following the fox, it's clear it is leading these hunters into a trap that could injure or kill. If the players warn the hunters, the fox will rebuke them for ruining its fun.

90 The players find a statue of a bride and of a groom, both lying on the ground as if they had been carelessly tossed there. If the players stand the statues under the arch, eerie music plays and ghostly shapes appear to attend the wedding. Performing the wedding rites for the two statues will break the spell as the two are brought back to life.

91 A creek that runs through the forest starts at a waterfall that is falling from a small stone island that hovers high in the air. Investigating the island reveals a small lake formed from a magical bottle endlessly pouring into the lake. If the players cork the bottle, the water will stop flowing, and eventually the lake will dry up.

92 Around a tree are small dolls made from twigs and leaves that resemble the players. Each player looking at their dolls sees a message saying "This one will betray you all," and an arrow points at one of the other's dolls. Each player sees the same message, but the arrow points at a different doll.

93 The players find ruins of what was once a vast castle. Searching around reveals an ancient scroll that tells of a great calamity that was coming. The king of the castle cast a spell to keep everyone safe until the calamity ended. There are scraps of the spell, which can be used to call them back, lying around the ruins.

94 Up ahead the players can see a treasure chest stuck deep in the mud, but the way the trees have fallen and the moss has grown, it looks like it is in the middle of a giant alligator's open maw. It is, in fact, a giant alligator.

95 Lately, the group has noticed lots of animals in this forest that are not known species here. Eventually, they come upon a broken-down circus caravan. The ringleader begs you to find and capture their lost acts.

96 The trees in this part of the swamp are actually giant heron legs, and two giant beaks smash down at the players. Clearly, the herons think the players are a tasty treat.

97 The players find a small bird sitting on a large rock. The bird can speak and tells the players that it's waiting for this egg to hatch.

98 This whole section of the swamp is covered in cattails. The strange brown bulbs feel extra solid and dense. When the wind picks up, the cattails start swaying, bludgeoning anyone who is in this field of plants.

99 A lithe black cat jumps from dead branch to dead branch while tracking the players through the swamp. The cat keeps a good distance and watches their every move. If anyone gets too close, the cat sprouts bat wings and flies to a safe distance. It's a flying cat and nothing more.

100 Swords, shields, spears, and broken banners litter this section of the swamp. Historians know that a major battle happened in this area many, many years ago. As the players pass, skeletons rise out of the mud and grab these weapons to attack the players.

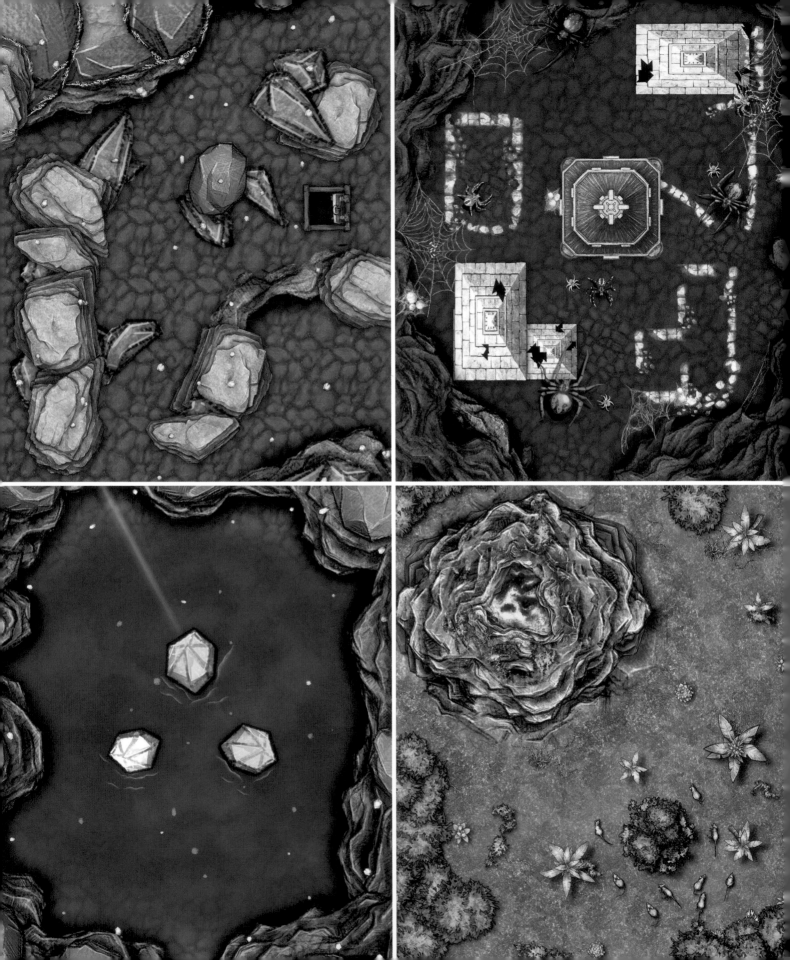

UNDERGROUND/CAVE

Encounters hidden underground beneath the earth tend to focus on the strange creatures and people adapted to an alien landscape. Tightening, widening, and branching passages provide the perfect excuse to get the players lost. From marveling at vast underground worlds to stumbling blindly through dark caverns filled with terrifying creatures, your players will wander through these spaces until they are finally reunited with the warm embrace of the sun.

One fun way to play up those oddities is to show why the people and creatures the players meet call this place home. From aboveground outcasts to born-and-bred underworld residents, these NPCs represent a different way of life to the party.

This setting translates well into stories of overconfidence—of digging too deep. Brain-draining cephalopods, elemental monstrosities, and Lovecraftian horrors can feel out of place elsewhere, but can find a natural home in your campaign deep beneath the earth.

1 A wrong turn leads the players into a hall of mirrored stalactites and stalagmites. Some of the mirrors belong to a giant with sharpened, chromed teeth!

2 The players discover a trail of golden coins leading deeper underground. As they follow the trail of coins, the players are caught in a huge cage dropped on them by a gigantic golden dragon. Having captured several groups of adventurers along with the players, she's assembled enough teams for her deadly competition game show.

3 The players turn a corner deep underground and find themselves in an idyllic coastal village whose exceptionally welcoming residents invite you to a feast. In reality, your players are still underground, hypnotized by brain leachers.

4 This large open cavern is the meeting hall of a council of dragons that meets once a year. They mistake the players for messengers bringing them news and demand that the players present their findings to the council immediately.

5 A reformed brain leacher wants to give up siphoning brain juice as sustenance and live on the surface. He asks the players to convince the nearby village that he isn't too dangerous to hang out with.

6 A figure burrows up from the ground shouting "Run! It's the Wodgian Wizard of the Worms." The abyss worm they've been nursing has now fully recovered. Everyone needs to get far away from here or be transported to the abyss by way of the worm's digestive track. After they escape, the wizard offers a card with their picture on it. This card can call abyss worms to the surface.

7 A cave-in threatens to trap the players if they don't act fast to stop the falling debris.

8 After bargaining with a fly-like individual in this bog, things begin changing about anyone who bought or sold anything from or to the merchant. Their appearance is slowly changing to look like a fly.

9 This cave contains skeletons arranged in an awkward but seemingly deliberate pattern. Upon closer inspection, the group can feel heat radiating from the fallen figures. With harrowing clicks, clacks, and pops, all the bones rise up together to make one terrifying bone golem!

10 A room filled with mushrooms makes the players a bit loopy. The spores here put them into a nightmarish trance where they must fend off giant, carnivorous mushrooms.

11 Colorful glass adorns the walls of this room. The lighting gives it a beautiful, eerie glow. This is a sanctuary for some unknown religion. The place is deserted, but remnants of books and pamphlets describe a cult dedicated to a great god.

12 The players find the only cave for miles to escape a harsh and cold rain. Unfortunately, the cave is already occupied by a massive bear.

13 This cavern is lined with a series of stalagmites that are giving off steam, making this whole area hot and damp. The steam coalesces into strange steam imps who resent the players' intrusion.

14 The tunnel opens up to a large cavern with two more branching tunnels. There's a battle between two warring deep gnome clans, and you've wound up right in the crossfire!

15 Following a river through a set of caves leads the players to the top of an underground waterfall, overlooking a hidden cove deep within this mountain. A large pirate ship is docked here. Rowdy singing can be heard from a building on the shore.

16 Gopherfolk have lots of tunnels here but don't allow outsiders to use them. If the players can get on these people's good side, the tunnel network offers shortcuts to almost anywhere.

17 A chamber here is sealed with a giant door engraved with a hammer and skull. Inside, short stone coffins line the walls. This is the den of a dwarven vampire brood. There is stirring inside the coffins.

18 A massive rock in this room seems to move whenever no one is looking directly at it. Unfortunately, it moved with one of the players on top of it. How will the others find their friend again in this mysterious cavern?

19 The cave here looks like an underground pub. This pub's usual clientele are denizens of the underground, so the players may get some curious looks.

20 The players discover a small, very secure home. Inside are four cult members who are astonished to see you. They believed all life was destroyed in a great calamity years ago. Their leader said she was sacrificing herself to save them, then locked them inside this cave home. She actually just stole all their possessions and now lives comfortably on the surface.

21 The players discover a small community of goblins for whom gravity is reversed. They didn't notice the goblins casually walking along the ceiling, but now the goblins are furious that the players entered their home without asking. They're even angrier that the players are tracking dirt all over the ceiling!

22 This cavern ends in a sharp cliff edge. At the far end of a narrow footbridge is the home of an elderly kobold. He invites the players for tea and swaps adventuring stories.

23 You've uncovered an abandoned transit system built by some long-dead civilization. Its only inhabitants are roaming packs of voles—descendants of a species once domesticated by the locals. They are impressed by feats of strength, and may join the players if a member can best them in unarmed combat.

24 A massive, painted cave mural shows a map of all known tunnels in the area! Some tunnels have labels. Of those, some have skulls, some have money signs, and some have both.

25 A dwarf has been experimenting with cultivating hops that can grow underground. He thought his first batch was successful, but his bar patrons have been showing signs of a strange illness and seem to have something growing on their skin.

26 Impossibly large ribs decorate the roof of this part of the cave. They're from some long-deceased behemoth...or that's what the party assumes, until they wade into acidic digestive juices!

27 Small holes in the sides of the cave have begun appearing with more and more frequency. A few minutes later, the players notice that the floor is unstable from all these holes.

28 This cave suddenly empties into a giant labyrinth of coffins, macabre art, and Gothic architecture. The players swear they hear rustling, knocking, and ominous whispers every now and then, but dismiss it as nerves.

29 The players stumble upon a glittering mine of crystals...but upon further inspection, it's a horde of gem spiders! Could still sell for a lot if captured though.

30 The players find a vein of cursed fool's gold and the accursed miners taken in by its allure. They mine and mine and mine without taking a break.

31 Just inside the cave entrance is a mining cart with seating. Sitting in the cart takes the passengers on a wild roller-coaster ride through the cave system. At the end, a deep gnome waits to be paid for the entertainment.

32 Embedded in the walls of this cave are gemstones commemorating the lives of people who have died. Touching a gemstone replays a bit of their life and their memories. Curiously, one of the players touches a gem, and memories of their own life play back to them.

33 All the citizens in this mining colony are digging with whatever implements they have. It's not clear what they are digging for. A powerful entity is controlling their minds in an attempt to be released from its prison far underground.

34 Large spiked creatures are forcing smaller creatures here to mine for precious gems in the rock wall. The big creatures are equipped with weaponry, and the smaller creatures are covered in scars.

35 A group of miners runs through tunnels, chasing something the players only catch glimpses of. The miners explain they are chasing the Silver Woman, a being made of solid silver. She seems amused by the chase.

36 The walls here are covered in majestic, glowing multicolored stones. Closer inspection reveals each stone holds elemental magic capable of casting spells. Disturbing the stones, however, causes the walls to shake, and earth, wind, fire, and air elemental guardians attack the players to scare them off.

37 Upon walking into this area, the adventurers fall through a trapdoor into a minecart where their legs are shackled in. They are stuck on a looping track through this mine while being swiped and sniped at by unseen creatures in the dark.

38 The players disturb a nest of bats that immediately swarm them all, biting and scratching before flying out of the cave to safety.

39 The players come to a dead end. There's a sign that points down, a drawing of treasure, then some handwriting that says "Shhh, it's a secret!" If the players dig down 30 feet, they find a treasure chest.

40 An eerie purple glow draws the group's attention. This cavern is filled with mortiferous crystals. The crystals are valuable as poison and used in anti-venoms, but it's dangerous to breathe the air around them for too long.

41 The walls and floors of this cavern are covered in gemstones with clear gnaw marks. Hiding in the small alcove, a small, cute gremlin is happily eating a few broken gemstones. The gremlin waves at the players. If they convince the gremlin to join them, it will always try to eat any gems they find.

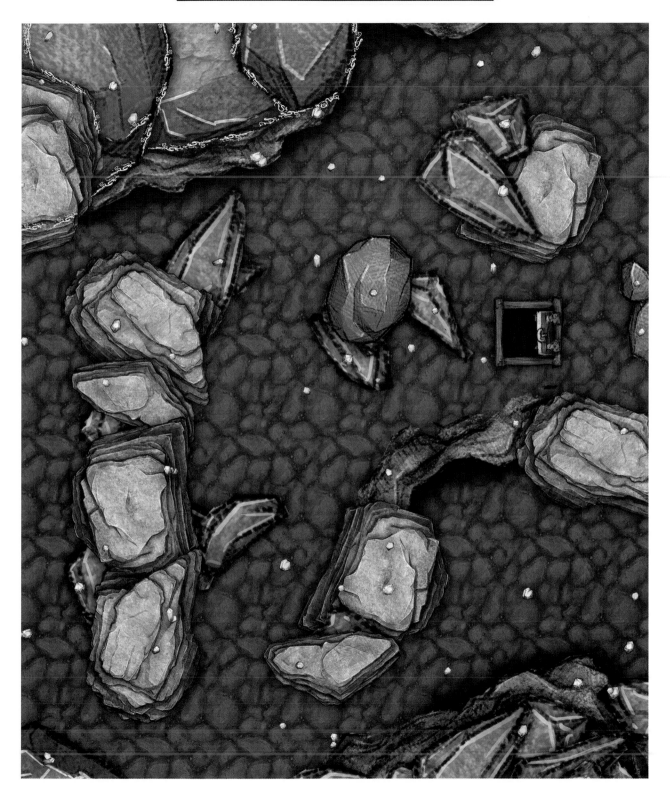

42 The cave structure suddenly opens up to a huge golden city. Atop a tall building in the center of the city, a dwarf is holding a golden idol. If the idol touches the skin of any character, they turn to gold as well. If the idol is taken from the figure, the dwarves return to life and demand the idol be returned, even as the golden curse begins to fade from the city.

43 The players scavenged a meal from things they found in the cave, but they put something bad in the meal, because everyone wakes up in a cozy dwelling, being nursed back to health by a very kind giant spider. The spider makes sure they have a hot meal and are in tip-top shape before they move on.

44 The players enter an underground city, but the entrance and exit are quickly cut off by the annual Night Day Parade of the Mole People. Interrupting the parade incurs the elder moles' wrath, so it's probably best to join in.

45 The players discover a lost, abandoned city. A crumbling but still magically animated guardian statue interprets the players as intruders and defends its city. After dealing with the statue, make a connection between the city and one of your player's backstories.

46 The group runs headfirst into a web spanning the width of the cave. Any bare skin in contact with the web begins to burn. Tentacles emerge from holes near the ends of the web, grasping for the players trapped in the web.

47 A tone that's been audible for a while now is quickly becoming unbearably loud and ear-piercing. It seems to be coming from the cave itself.

48 Off in the distance of this large cavern sits a castle that is upside down, hanging from the ceiling. There is a caretaker who moves through the castle like it was right side up. The lonely caretaker offers to enchant them so they can explore the castle, but the effect will last a full week.

49 Loose dirt on the cave floor begins to shake as the whir of drill beetles gets louder. The beetles make this sound when their nest has been threatened.

50 This tunnel opens onto a vast Dwarf City. Unfortunately, it looks like it's been taken over by spiderfolk. They've killed or bound many of the dwarves and now turn their attention to the players.

51 This tunnel opens up to a huge cavern filled with treasure. Just as the group is rummaging through the loot, a dragon's roar can be heard in the distance.

52 A vast, underground city looks mostly abandoned. As the players explore, they may notice a few moving shadows. Eventually it becomes obvious they are being stalked by a group of ravenous vampires.

53 A bass beat rumbles the players' chests as the Elite Assassins Dance Troupe vogues onto the scene in this under-underground club. They are well known for challenging groups to a dance-off. They kill anyone they deem inferior.

54 A partly burned, crumbling journal is found on the ground, splattered with blood. It tells of an expedition with high hopes of finding the "source of sorrow" from local legend. The journal gets more and more dire until the entries end abruptly. A clicking sound that was barely audible when the group started reading the journal can now be heard clearly emanating from the darkness ahead.

55 This underground lake fills the entire cavern. The only way across is by swimming or taking a boat. Luckily, a deep gnome is sitting next to a boat with a big grin and a hand outstretched for payment.

56 The walls of this cavern are studded with precious gemstones. Three crystal pillars form a large triangle in the center of the room. A closer look shows some type of humanoid is trapped in each of the crystal pillars.

57 The waters in this underground lake are crystal clear. At the bottom of the lake are rows and rows of stone statues all with their faces looking up and back at the players. A whispered voice from somewhere says, "This army can be yours. Let's make a deal."

58 This cavern's walls look like the inside of a geode with small crystals jutting out everywhere. In the center of the ceiling a small hole lets in light that strikes one of three large crystals in the center of the room. Each of these large crystals is able to turn and focus the light, but to what end?

59 This underground lake gives off a faint glow, making the whole cavern dance with an eerie light. Within the lake are many schools of fish giving off a bioluminescent glow.

60 Three large crystals dominate the center of this room, each about 5 feet apart from each other. A faint humming can be heard from each. Faint tracks on the ground suggest that the crystals can be pushed closer together, and when they are, the humming gets louder.

61 A small crystal creature approaches the players. It appears to be a baby...of some unknown species. It seems extremely fragile. If the players don't protect it, they fear it will be shattered.

62 The players are traveling downward when they begin to hear a song. It's faint but gradually grows. It's coming from crystals in the wall. If taken out of the wall, a crystal stops singing, and the music of the other crystals becomes more melancholy.

63 This room is ankle-deep in water that laps up against three large crystals that dominate this room. A party of deep dwarves steps forward and demands that the players leave because they have claimed this rock candy as theirs.

64 The players find a small underground lake. The bottom of the lake is littered with copper and silver coins. A small dragon-like creature swims out to confront them.

65 This odd underground forest is barely surviving. The dryads of the trees are dying and close to madness. The few fairies that are left are hyperprotective of the few things that are still living but can be reasoned with if the players have an excellent idea to help.

66 The area shakes as a strange contraption with a drill on the front plows through the wall. It screeches to a halt just before hitting the players. A gnome with wild hair and goggles pops out of the vehicle. They yell at the players that they "coulda gotten killed!"

67 The underground path opens up to an enormous cavern that looks to be a jungle. A small volcano in the center of the cavern seems to be providing heat and some light to the area. Suddenly a pack of giant rats bursts from the brush being chased by a tyrannosaurus.

68 All manner of species flock to this underground hot spring. If the players want to rest here, an assistant asks them to set an intention before entering the waters. The waters heal all internal and external wounds, and leave a lasting positive effect that reflects the set intention of each individual.

69 At the center of this cavern is what looks to be a volcano or a geyser. Suddenly the mound rumbles and bolts of electricity shoot out of the "geyser," showering the ceiling with electrical charges. Large bats made of lightning drop from the ceiling and attack the players.

70 This area has many exotic specimens of mushrooms, including one that spews deadly spores if disturbed. If the adventurers want to get through, they'll have to be extremely careful.

71 The players find themselves in a strange underground jungle filled with unusual birds and animals. A tribe of deep elves surrounds the party and questions them on why they have come to their sanctuary and nature preserve.

72 The floor collapses, and the players fall into a strange underground jungle. They land on the head of a gigantic frog that is very cross about the lump on its head. It attacks with a huge tongue!

73 There is a small cult living underground after their prophet predicted the end of the world. They think the players are apocalypse demons.

74 This massive cavern is full of dead trees with bodies hanging from them. Behind all the trees is a dark stone manor house that is barely perceptible, the foul home of the lich Alabaster Dred. Dred uses all the dead bodies hanging from the trees and those he has buried to weaken the players before taking them on himself.

75 A large bug person has set up shop here, selling detailed maps of the area. The maps have an incredible amount of information, and what looks like an additional layer of info about these places that the players can't quite comprehend.

76 The players begin sweating as the temperature gets hotter. A large cavern opens up and seems to be ablaze with light and heat. A horned humanoid sits leisurely in a lava pit. They offer wish fulfillment for terrible prices.

77 Lush fauna is somehow growing here despite the lack of sunlight. Purple primates of a sort are battling each other with various glowing weapons. When they notice the players, the weapons turn toward these new intruders in their land.

78 The players find an abandoned forge that seems to have been fed by a lava tube. If the players can get the forge working again, a mystic blacksmith appears and can make them one item.

79 Ahead is a very deep and wide chasm. Strange stones float in the air as a path across the gap. When touched, the stones move. One can try to timidly move across by trying to balance on the floating stones, or confidently march across, and the stones will fly up to meet their feet.

80 A series of stalagmites shoots scalding water into the air at random intervals, making everything slick. Those clever enough to notice the pattern of the water spouts can time it just right to avoid getting burned.

81 A dwarven cave-farmer couple has an impressive mushroom garden in this area. The men seem perfectly content living off the land here. "The only thing settin' us back would be the Dread Gophers we gotta chase off with our axes! You wouldn't mind riddin' us of the varmints, would ya?"

82 This large grotto is an open-air market selling items from around the world. Runes placed around the area prevent fighting and magic spells from working. Things turn dangerous when it is discovered that one of the runes has been destroyed.

83 Cave dwarves have set up shop in this area. One can buy stale bread, rock bread, or unbreakable bread. All come with a satisfaction guarantee! The cave dwarf baker guarantees the unbreakable bread "will stand up to even the heartiest of swords!"

84 A large cavern is ringed by a narrow pathway leading deeper into the hole. In the center of the cavern is the 200-foot-tall statue of a horrific creature bound by thick chains. A group of hooded creatures is trying to break through the chains binding this statue.

85 A pool of lava is 500 feet beneath the ridge the players are on. A series of giant, thick chains extend from the wall to a small island being held aloft in the center of the cavern. On that island sits the prison their friend is being held in.

86 The opening of this large cave system is called the gauntlet. The players are competing to get to the end of the caves and defeat the final creature inside to win 10,000 gold pieces. There are three paths to choose from, with different challenges and obstacles for each path. All the teams are sent in at the same time, so the players have to deal with the monsters inside and with the other teams trying to sabotage their progress.

87 This underground town, called The Cracks, has beautiful and unusual homes and buildings carved into the rock walls. The Cracks is home to everyone who has fallen through the cracks in society: those who don't fit in or have been driven out.

88 The cavern ahead is covered in snow, frost, and ice. In the center of the cavern a white glowing orb pulses, sending out waves of cold. Four large white wolves step out from the shadows to protect the orb.

89 The natural flooring of this tunnel turns to cobblestone as it leads to a bridge. Over the bridge is a small town square and a few buildings with lights in the windows. This is the guard post on the border of a large underground kingdom, and the elves stationed here demand to know the players' business within the city. Convincing the guards results in getting papers that allow players to move freely for a short amount of time. Failure causes the guards to attack.

90   This large cavern has three giant skulls carved into the far wall, from floor to ceiling. Each skull is carved with unique designs. In the mouth of each skull is a locked door. Ancient golems stand motionless in front of each door.

91   One player is abducted from the back of the group without the rest of the party noticing. Take that player out of the room and let them know they have been put under a silence spell and need to get a message to the group about their whereabouts.

92   The players enter a strange room of deep red crystals. By touching the crystals, they get glimpses of an ancient civilization. Each crystal is a diary entry that the players can experience. This ancient society had some incredible technology.

93   The floor here has a large unfinished magic circle painted on it. At the far side of the room is a gnome whose hands have been broken. She says that Alabaster Dred, a lich, trapped her down here and broke her hands before she could complete the magic circle to teleport out. She begs the players to finish the circle so she can get them all out before Dred returns.

94   The sound of fast-running water in the darkness suggests that an underground river is nearby. Glowing fish are attempting to swim upstream. A party of underground elves arrives and demands that the party leave their hunting and fishing grounds or die.

95   An intricate root structure is visible on the walls here. Venturing farther, the roots get denser, reaching subtly out toward the players. Some skulls of various sizes of animals can be seen mixed into the roots. These "roots" are actually a brain-eating fungus attempting to prey on anyone or anything passing by.

96   At the shore of this underground river is a simple boat and a skeletal boatman. The skeleton points to the river and the hundreds of waterlogged, undead hands that are grasping up at the surface. It then points at the boat and waits. It holds the only paddles and will fight if necessary.

97   This cavern is filled with giant, colorful, glowing mushrooms—red, blue, yellow, and purple. Each cluster is tall enough for the players to stand underneath. At the far end of the room, four beacons randomly light up, filling the room with painful light effects. Red causes the players to burn, blue freezes, yellow electrifies, and purple poisons. Standing under the correct mushroom color will protect against these effects.

98   These tunnels are littered with stalactites and stalagmites that look to have tiny windows carved into them and lights coming out. Anyone who looks in these windows is accosted by angry rock pixies that don't like being spied on. They call for pixie swarms to drive the players away.

99   This stretch of tunnel has tiles of a variety of colors on the floor. Similarly colored crystals hang from the ceiling and emit light in a specific pattern once every twenty minutes. The pattern of the crystal flashes tells the safe path across the floor. Any misstep causes a massive electrical shock.

100   The temperature drops as the party goes deeper inside; they eventually come upon an ice wall with figures frozen inside. The figures are some kind of horrific, many-legged creatures with humanoid hands at the end of each leg. That's when the party realizes this is a bombipede nest. When startled, bombipedes explode, potentially thawing the ice wall!

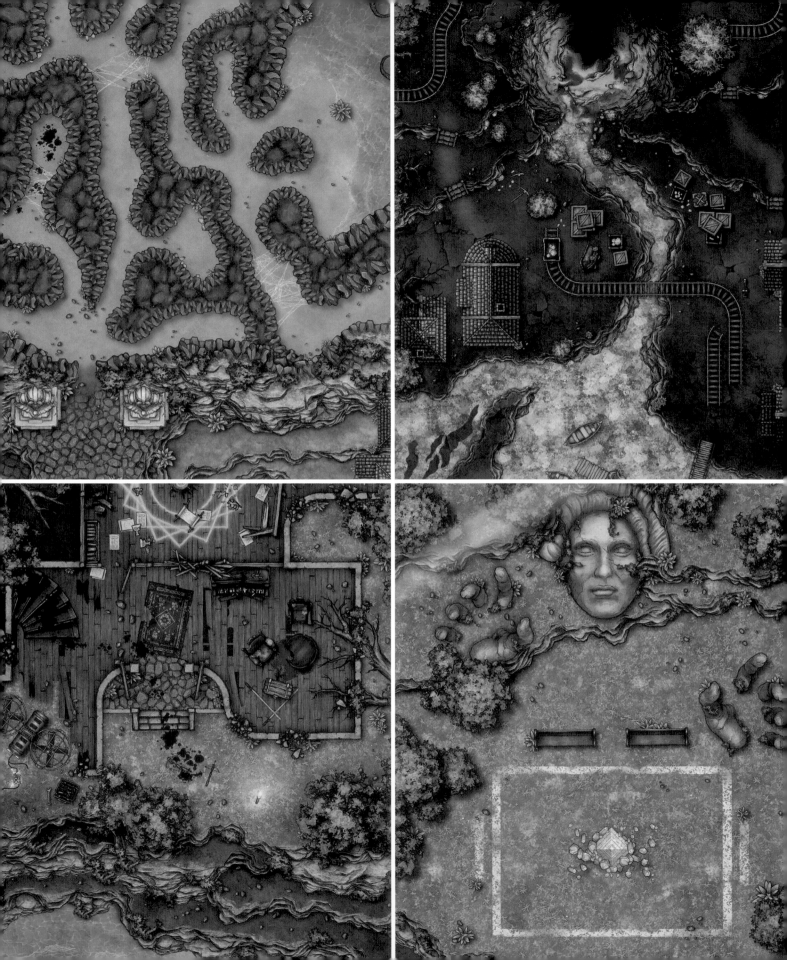

MOUNTAINS

On a mountain, you can expect to find just about anything, and it's the best spot for acrobatic action. Not only does the fall provide built-in stakes, but the remoteness of the mountain can also make even a minor wound into a major problem. Safe places for R&R are few and far between. Even when you find that cozy cave, make sure to check it for yetis first!

It's not all avalanches and obstacle courses though. Elementals, trolls, and abominable creatures of all kinds can populate your combat encounters up here. There are even giants, if your party's confident enough! Of course, maybe you'll find a way to make friends with them instead.

As for what types of social encounters to expect, the mountain is a great home for oddball outsiders. Wise hermits are right at home, but so are industrious dwarves, monastic orders, and beastfolk. After all, the mountain is your best bet if you want to make sure you're not ever bothered by rowdy city slickin' types!

1　A mad genius has finally set up a series of large lenses that she plans to use to harness the sun to rain fire upon all the nearby villages and cities.

2　A sudden sound signals that an avalanche has started above the group. They have mere minutes to find a way to survive the oncoming snow.

3　An ancient-looking monk walks effortlessly up the face of the mountain and acknowledges the players.

4　A giant yeti appears, pulling out a gnarled wooden board. "I've got a sack full of gold for anyone who can beat me down the hill!" it shouts before snowboarding away.

5　After riding out a snowstorm under a mountain overhang, the players step out into a village made of snow. Strange wintry fairies are busily rolling up snow into balls and storing them in one of the ice houses. If the players approach, one of the larger fairies steps in and blocks their path.

6　A nest on a small cliff above has around a dozen eggs that appear to be golden. If the party waits a while, solid gold birds flit to the nest and fly off again.

7　A god sits on the side of the mountain. Not an aspect, not an avatar, an in-person god. They are in the mood to play, and make a deal that if you can amuse them, they will grant you a boon.

8　The path on this section of the mountain is so thin that the players can only walk single file. The rocks are also unfortunately slick from sleet and snow.

9　The ruins of a village are covered in ice and snow. A search of the place turns up no life, but carved into one of the walls is a dire warning to leave this place lest the ice demon claim them too. As the party searches, a dark and evil laugh echoes through the town.

10　A gigantic, snow-colored ape climbs up from the opposite side of the mountain and, with a giant roar, attempts to grab one of the players, then jumps to the peak.

11　A chill goes through the air as giant fingers are formed by snowfall. Some kind of weather god is displeased by something and is taking it out on anyone currently climbing this mountain.

12　High in the mountain, in a natural valley, there is a golden palace with a beautiful garden. Inside resides a wide diversity of people and creatures who have left society behind to pursue a higher truth. They defend their home with their lives if needed, but are friendly as long as any visitors swear an oath to keep this secret or stay with them.

13　A winter storm forces the players to find shelter in a strange fortress carved into the mountainside. This fortress is a prison that has long been forgotten, and the people who live here are the original prisoners' descendants who long to be set free.

14　Players discover the ruins of a lost civilization. The architecture is ornate, crumbling, and covered in the faded art of forgotten gods and kings. Within the ruins, grave robbers are stealing artifacts.

15　A ski lift–type mechanism can be seen going up the mountain, but strangely, it goes up beyond the peak into the sky. You can't see where it ends.

16 A man with an enormous beard snores loud enough to be audible from outside his cabin in the mountain. He accidentally took too much sleeping potion the last time he went to bed, and he's finally waking up. He's been asleep for two hundred years.

17 A looking lens is set up on the edge of a cliff. If a player uses the lens, they can see miles away, but are also immediately transported to any location they look at for five seconds or more. This is a one-way trip.

18 A sign points up the trail stating "Jaggie's Mystical Spa Ahead." At the end of the trail is a bright-eyed gnome in front of a set of hot springs. She is Jaggie and gives access to the hot springs, a towel, and one drink, all for 1 gold.

19 The Parched Raven, a tavern balanced on the top of this mountain's peak, has a reputation for catering to unsavory clientele. This would be a great place to hire a killer or get stabbed in a poker game. Patrons here know lots of secrets, but anyone looking for information should keep their queries discreet.

20 A cave in the cliffside is filled with barrels of glowing green liquid. Some of the players may be able to tell that the substance is Rotgut, a potent intoxicant. It's illegal in most large cities and sells for quite a lot in those same places (if you can find a buyer).

21 The bridge over this chasm rotted away long ago with the strands of the old bridge dangling in the deep. It looks possible to jump but it's risky. A clever gnome approaches, offering to sell them her instant bridge-making device.

22 The players discover a palatial home on the side of the mountain, and the people who live there mistake them for the temporary servants they sent for to tend them on their two-week getaway. It's free room, food, and pay if the players can deal with the ever-increasing demands of the guests.

23 This once-fine lodge in the mountains was a famed getaway spot for the rich. It is now the home of a band of goblins who love to snowboard on the mountainside near their new lodge.

24 In the distance, the group notices a humongous, ancient corpse; it's somehow mostly preserved and nearly the size of the mountain itself. Have the players take turns each telling what their character knows about this dead titan.

25 There is a horde of strange, aggressive, colorful creatures in four groups: yellow, red, blue, and purple. The area's lighting changes color—from red to blue to yellow—every ten seconds. The monsters are immune to attacks unless the light shining on them matches their color. The light never seems to turn purple!

26 A temple on a tall mountain peak is filled with all manner of creatures devoting their time and worship to a "new god of the heights." The leader here welcomes the group to have a warm meal and a soft bed, provided, of course, that they swear devotion to this new god.

27 A small child is lost in the mountains. She wears noble children's clothes, beyond tattered from her journey. She ran away from her home to find her older brother, who also ran away from home into the mountains. Do the players send her back home or help her look?

28 This maze in the mountains is guarded by two massive stone statues. The statues animate upon approach and warn anyone attempting to enter the maze to turn around. If ignored, they will attack.

29 One of the players is bitten by a deadly snake. Someone in the party may know that an antidote can be made from a purple and pink flower that grows "at the last grass before snow on a mountain peak."

30 A figure in a brown cloak excitedly introduces themself as the Wodgian Wizard of the Wold. They've used mountain-shaping magic to make a canyon maze filled with deadly earth elementals. Unfortunately, no one wants to play-test the labyrinth. If the party can get out of the maze, the wizard offers a card with their picture on it. This spell card can reshape any 300-square-foot area into a complex maze.

31 A terrified gnome runs out of a cliffside cave carrying a throbbing crystal. They explain, "If we don't get this into my polarity flanger in the next hour, this mountain is dust." The polarity flanger is miles away.

32 The players enter a canyon maze with high ceilings. Once they've made a few turns and are sufficiently within the maze, hooded archers appear on the top of the maze walls and attempt to pick them off.

33 A herd of Pegasuses is resting quietly high in these mountains; they are curious but cautious about the players.

34 A monk sits atop a stone alongside this mountain path. As the players pass them, they suggest that the path ahead is too deadly. The monk offers the players a place to stay for the night while the danger passes for nothing more than some good company.

35 Dwarves have cut a pass through this large mountain range and have built their vast city into the walls that run along it. The city has become a major center of trade, as it is the easiest way through the mountains. It is also often under attack by nations that would like to control that pass.

36 A small misstep sends the players toppling down the side of the mountain. They're able to regain their footing, but realize their supplies have fallen much farther down, through a treacherous cleft in the mountain.

37 The only way farther up the pass is blocked by a bunch of angry mountain goats that clearly don't want you in their territory.

38 Steps lead down into a canyon maze. The players will have to hurry because there is a huge storm quickly filling the maze with murky water. To make matters worse, some of the characters notice with terror that they can feel tentacles attempting to grab their feet.

39 The players begin struggling to continue. They have traveled high enough that oxygen is in short supply. If they want to continue, they'll need a solution for how they will continue breathing.

40 This part of the mountain is covered in a strange fungus. The fungus attempts to capture anyone who walks through it and dissolves them in the nearby hot springs for sustenance.

41 A large pile of stones looks too strange to be naturally caused. Hidden in the mound is a sealed barrel. A note attached reads "Broadstone emergency supplies for Broadstone family members only. All others will be CURSED." The note looks to have been written by a child.

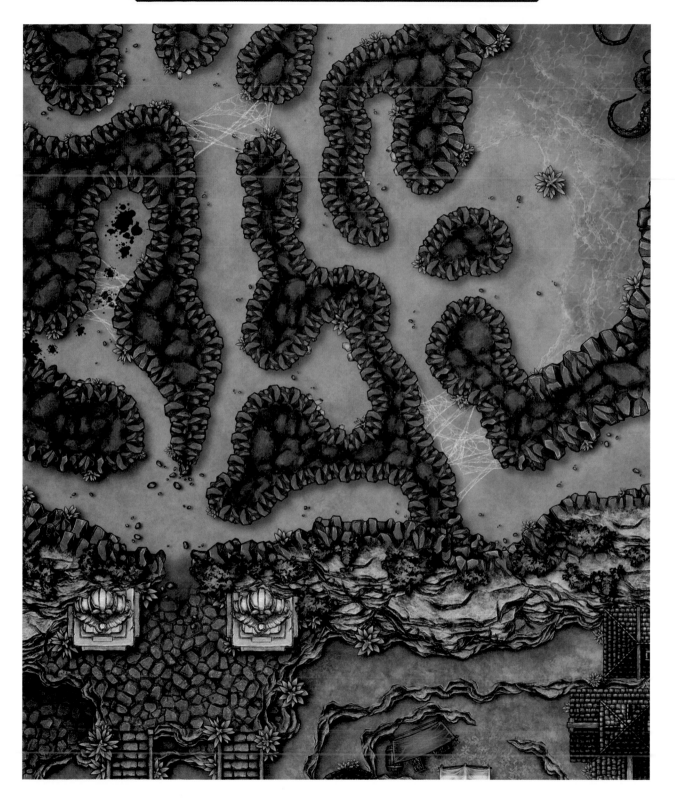

THE LAKE OF FIRE

42 A village of gnomes and dwarves has built an industrial city on the edge of an active volcano and uses the heat for many ingenious purposes. However, there's a dragon in the center of that volcano and it's about to wake up.

43 This section of the mountain has become compromised due to volcanic activity. Jump to safety or be burned alive!

44 This natural hot spring seemed like a perfect place to rest, but the sight of the scaly back of some large creature moving easily beneath the surface is definitely unnerving.

45 A troupe of dwarves has found a way to sail upon a molten lake of lava. They invited the party to go fishing but are attacked by the strange things that live in the fire.

46 A band of goblins is trying to boil a large egg within the pool of a natural hot spring. Off in the distance, the loud screech of a bird can be heard. The goblins will fight off anyone trying to steal their feast.

47 The ground shudders, cracks, then crumbles. The players are falling into the mountain's internal cave structure. It's 100 feet down. What do they do to slow their fall?

48 The cold mountain air suddenly turns blazing hot. The snow melts underfoot as the ground cracks open. A lava flow bursts from the ground and an enormous salamander flops out. It's agitated, and belching up lava.

49 This mountain is actually a volcano that is suddenly erupting. Not only is lava coming out, but strange fire monsters are also spilling out and attacking anything they see.

50 A town full of people made out of fire has built a village around the rim of an active volcano. They are willing to trade their specialty goods, but the heat makes it hard for anyone to stay in the village for long.

51 This castle in the mountains has a moat of lava with two fire demons swimming in it keeping watch. Whoever's inside clearly doesn't wish to be disturbed.

52 A guidepost and accompanying trail sign tells of a truly incredible view at the end of a long trek through lava caverns, gravel spider nests, and a part of the trail that has a skull drawn on it.

53 Heavily armored dwarves guard the way forward. They keep dropping hints that they need to practice for their upcoming lava polo match. The dwarves will gladly let them pass if the players play a round. Lava polo is played on the back of trained salamanders that can swim through the nearby volcano crater.

54 A deep chasm splits the path ahead of the players. From down in the darkness, a voice can be heard calling for help. Whoever it is fell in and is stuck.

55 Dwarves are sunning themselves on the shores of a lava pool. It seems like it's dwarf spring break here. The dwarves are playing volleyrock, lava polo, and just generally letting it all hang out.

56   The path leads to an invisible wall that when touched overrides a person's senses. When they come to, they find they have walked back down the path a long way. Only the most intelligent can resist this wall and pass through to find an ancient library full of wonders.

57   This large cliffside house is the home of a team of dwarves and gnomes who are trying to make a new type of flying machine with little success. Some think their project is cursed, but the head of the project believes that someone on the team is sabotaging their efforts.

58   The journey becomes perilous, as there are few safe footholds on the side of the mountain. The players need to think about how they will avoid falling to their deaths. The way ahead will mean lots of long jumps and climbing.

59   A cliffside house nearby is being swarmed by what look like pterodactyls. Inside, a family is attempting to fend off the creatures as best they can, to little effect.

60   Yelling can be heard around the corner. It's a family reunion of several dwarf clans: Beardaxe, Beardsword, Bêar'd'hamm'r, and Beardnyspears. They are having a fierce argument over which weapons are the best. When they see the players, they implore them to settle this debate once and for all.

61   A very old person stands outside of a door looking expectantly toward it, wide-eyed and hopeful. They tell the players they are waiting for the door to open, and it should happen any second now. Anyone looking directly at the door is pulled toward it and wishes to wait eagerly for its inevitable opening.

62   In a strange mansion, an order of holy knights protects an artifact that is the legendary key to defeating an ancient evil. Everyone believes that the evil was defeated ten years ago. But was it really?

63   There is a huge earthquake that topples the players to the ground. A chunk of mountain about a mile in diameter (including where the players are standing) suddenly floats up and away from the earth. This section of mountain is now flying in the air, too far up to safely jump down.

64   A house on the cliffside seems abandoned. The entrance is booby-trapped with a poison that makes anyone who breathes it in see terrible nightmare creatures that can do real mental harm. An evil chemist lives here experimenting on anyone they catch with the trap.

65   The sun is setting near the top of the mountain and there's a meteor shower. Some creatures seem to be peering intently at the shooting stars, then they leap up and grab onto them, flying away. It seems this phenomenon can be used for fast travel.

66   The players find a large house and workshop deep in the mountains. Inside is a man who makes toys relentlessly and cannot stop. He states that the only way to break his curse is to find a way to deliver all of these toys to children, but he can't ever leave.

67   Neon colors from magical light fixtures serve as signage for The Bearded Lady, a dwarven drag bar built into the rock of the mountain. It's a tavern with all the expected amenities and a nightly performance from Shania Dunnat, Bridget Beardaxe, Ultima Weapon, and more!

68 A moving, shimmering rainbow ignites the sky. It's the annual return of The Color. Bright as the scene is, it darkens the mood, because everyone knows the Chromicidim will be coming to siphon the color and life from anyone foolish enough to stay on the mountain tonight.

69 The players awaken a giant. The giant finds these tiny people very fascinating and wants to play! But when your "play-mate" is that much bigger than you, the stakes are life and death.

70 A group of dwarves is having a fire pie-eating contest. They scoff at the idea that the players would be up to this spicy challenge. The winner gets a gold reward and a dozen dragon's breath pies. Dragon's breath pies are rumored to be so hot that you can literally breathe fire for a while after eating one.

71 The players crest a peak and are confronted by a massive face. If prodded, the giant will attempt not to react, or try to make it clear the players are bothering them. If provoked further, the giant will stand up and fight.

72 The mountain rumbles beneath the players. In the distance, one of the mountain's peaks opens up like a giant mouth. This mountain is alive! It seems fairly irritated that so many people and creatures are walking all over it.

73 A ranger begins whisper-shouting at the group. They're apparently trespassing on Giant Peak territory. The ranger explains they'll need to leave quickly and quietly to the south.

74 As the players arrive at the top of this mountain, a solar eclipse is taking place. Once the sun is blocked, phantasmal figures appear everywhere! These creatures can be struck down, but when they are, another pops up nearby. The players will just need to survive until the eclipse is over.

75 A group of people is busy building many houses and structures out of snow and ice. They tell the players that they are preparing for a large group of scholars arriving soon to spend a week observing some strange atmospheric phenomenon. The scholars actually want to summon a creature from beyond the stars.

76 Dwarves are playing King of the Hill on this peak. It's a contact sport. Last one remaining standing and on the peak wins. If one of the players can win, there's a solid gold trophy in the shape of a mountain peak!

77 A group of extremely buff dwarves is playing a game they call "way high up" where they attempt to get an imposingly large boulder as high into the air as possible. The group scoffs at the players, not believing them capable of being "a true way-high-up baller."

78 A large, flat side of this mountain has been carved into some kind of game board with two huge stone paddles on the bottom. A nearby mountain gnome encourages you to try his pinboulder game: "Magic is allowed and encouraged! Just get a high score and you can have this magical flipper!"

79 A group of archaeologists has set up a dig site here, carving into the mountainside to uncover an enormous skeleton with many heads and limbs. The more the players talk to the digging crew, the weirder their responses get.

80 The Beardaxe dwarf clan runs a small business here, Beardaxe Beer and Axe Throwing. It sells libations popular throughout the world. The axe throwing has a daily scoreboard, and anyone who can make it to the top of the scoreboard gets free store credit!

81 A series of hot springs dots these cliffs high in the mountains. The smell of sulfur is almost unbearable, but many of the mountain's wildlife are peacefully bathing in the springs, oblivious to the foul stench.

82 A tall, luxurious but run-down hotel looms in the dip at the center of four peaks. The hotel owner's spirit is kindly, but most of the rooms have angry, and potentially deadly, spirits.

83 A group of boulder elementals is traveling down the mountain by rolling quickly. They don't seem to have much awareness for anything in their path, and they're headed directly toward the players.

84 As the players approach the bridge over the chasm, two giant hands reach up and snap it in two. A frightening and hungry-looking monster crawls out of the darkness and faces the party.

85 A small booth is set up selling hang gliders in various shapes and designs. For a small price, the players can have a new mode of transportation. The booth owner even knows wind magic, so they can give you a huge boost to begin your glide.

86 This town is built into the side of a caldera, which has filled in with water to become a natural lake. They aren't used to outsiders, since getting to this town is a long and treacherous journey.

87 Owlfolk have built a large structure here. They have a functioning village that is lifted into the air with large balloons. The people freely soar into and out of docks on these air platforms. This village is incredible, and clearly not designed for folks who can't fly.

88 In a small village nestled deep in the mountains, the villagers are celebrating the beginning of spring. Every home has a multitude of delicious baked goods and people in brightly colored masks are parading through the streets. The celebration takes a dark turn at night when the villagers begin looking for someone to fill the role of Old Man Winter, who will be burned at the stake at dawn.

89 A small cliff jutting out of the side of the mountain has a single tree growing on it and on that tree is a single gold pear. Getting to the pear without falling or causing the cliff to collapse is difficult. The pear is pure gold and will fetch a high price for any collector who has heard the myths.

90 At the foot of the mountain is an ogre and a goblin standing next to a giant slingshot with a sign that says "Willy and Billy's Fast Mountain Travel." The goblin, Willy, tells the players that for the small price of 25 gold, they will load them into the slingshot and fire them up the mountain. Each ride gets one feather that has feather fall cast on it for a safe landing. The feathers, however, are fake, and they just want to splat people into the side of a mountain and steal their stuff.

91 Carved into the sides of two mountains are two giant statues of human royalty with their hands stretched toward each other over a deep canyon. If the hands touched, it would be the shortest way to cross over the canyon, but there is about 50 feet separating the hands. Those who walk out on either arm will see a small plaque that says "Trust." There is an invisible force bridge between the two hands for those trusting enough to test.

92 The Beardsword dwarf clan is having its annual protect-the-cheese-wheel event. The rules are simple: Every team gets one giant cheese wheel that they have to protect as it rolls down the side of the mountain. Whoever has the most intact wheel at the bottom of the mountain wins 50 gold and a year's supply of ale and cheese.

93 A pack of winter wolves is hunting the mountain goats along this section of the mountain forest. The wolves may switch to the players if they seem easier to catch than the goats.

94 In a giant eagles' nest high in the mountains, there are two young eagles, and the parents are flying nearby. One of the baby eagles takes an immediate liking to one of the players and starts to get out of the nest and run to them. The giant eagle mother will swoop down and laugh if the players are being nice to the eagle and will speak to them about how funny the situation is. If the players are cruel, the eagles will attack.

95 The snowcap of this mountain hides a secret village made of ice and snow. A tribe of elves does its best to be welcoming. If the players wish to stay the night, one of the head elves tells them that they must earn their keep by helping their hunters hunt yeti out in the snow.

96 A large sleigh pulled by a team of six white wolves speeds impossibly down the side of the mountain toward the players. Small whirlwinds of snow form behind the sleigh as Silvaria the Snow Witch drives her team of wolves. She brings the sleigh to a halt and greets the players with a big smile. She wants to know what treasures they brought her.

97 A hunting party of wolverine-folk approaches the players through the rocks of the mountains. They demand to know if they have been hunting in their territory and they demand payment for taking their food. If not, they are willing to work with the party in hunting and escorting them through their territory.

98 A giant skeleton is leaning up against the side of the mountain, with an enormous sword sticking out of the mountainside roughly in the spot where the heart would have been. The area around the skeleton is littered with weapons and supplies. If the party is lucky, they will find a few magical items and weapons in the area.

99 A rushing river flows down the side of the mountain with a very strong current. A little farther up the mountain is a village full of minkfolk who are experts at fishing and logging. They have a bridge across the river but also will let the players ride a log down the fast-moving river for free!

100 The players walk into a cloud bank near the top of the mountain. As they exit the clouds, they find a castle and a number of giants wandering around tending to the cloud grounds while they have anchored to this mountain. These giants, hungry, all start sniffing around when the players are near.

ON THE ROAD

Ah, the open road! Don't you just love road trip movies? Knowing a story's destination means you've got something to look forward to at the end, and you get to have fun adventures along the way! When your party is traveling from one landmark to another, thinking about the journey on those terms can take travel sessions from feeling like a chore to being your favorite adventuring activity. As such, most of the encounters on this list lean into that spontaneity. They are encounters designed to be fun for a party just passing through, unlikely to revisit. Get in, have a fun adventure, get out. You've got other places to be. Along the way you'll likely encounter both fellow travelers and a fight or two—perhaps even at the same time! The variety in things you can find on a road adventure makes this setting great for balancing fights and chats.

In that spirit of variety, "on the road" might be one of the best settings in which you weave in some encounters from the downtime section later in this book. Many of those prompts feel (intentionally) a bit like icebreakers, which lend themselves to a road trip setting. As for specific types of stories that work well here, you can expect a decent amount of vehicle-based encounters, ambushes, and NPC interactions in small towns catering to travelers (including a tourist trap or two!). Highlighting a few of the scenes with different moods and levels of urgency like this makes your fictional journey feel more like a real one.

1 The group finds a wounded baby dragon. It won't survive on its own, but a baby dragon is a lot of responsibility! What will they do?

2 The mode of transportation breaks. How do the players fix this issue?

3 Each player chooses one character to have a scene with. The scene can be anything; it's just a time to learn more about your characters and how they feel about each other.

4 Seven swords are stuck into the ground next to the road in a crescent shape with a simple sign that says "Never forget." If someone takes a sword, they will slowly have their memories erased as the sword eats their mind. After seven days with the sword, a person will have completely forgotten who they are.

5 The group reaches a large town where the people all talk in a very old-fashioned way, and are dressed in clothes that would normally be seen only on the stage of a play about the ancient past. The townsfolk strongly encourage the players to rest there for the night. Turns out they're ghosts.

6 An ethereal group of animals beckons the players off the road. It seems a well-known fur merchant has a workshop near here. The animal spirits look scarred and tortured.

7 During the night, an abandoned fort is haunted by the regiment of soldiers who died defending it. The spirits will protect it from anyone in the vicinity unless they can achieve final rest.

8 The players come upon a lone skeleton walking along the side of the road, and the skeleton steps aside to allow the players to pass without incident. The skeleton carries a simple bag that looks stuffed full of odd items and a sword. If asked, they reply that they are returning home to complete a promise. The bag is full of personal items and mementos.

9 The players are enjoying a nice, sunny walk when, in the blink of an eye, they find themselves in the middle of the night, in the middle of a terrible storm. One bright light can be seen on top of a nearby hill. A large, decrepit house looms at the top.

10 The terrain gradually, almost imperceptibly, shifts to an otherworldly landscape. Giant purple mushrooms and a green sky let the players know they have accidentally ridden through some kind of portal to another realm.

11 Long vines have overgrown the road ahead, covering the next 400 feet at least. The vines look easily walked over, but when anything touches them, they attempt to wrap themselves around whatever they can and pull it off the road and into an enormous pitcher plant.

12 A large pile of leaves and sticks hides a pit trap in the middle of the road. The trap gives way when at least two people are standing on it. Once the trap is sprung, a haughty woman, her fanciful male companion, and their talking cat step out of hiding and demand all the players' rare items.

13 After a rogue kicked-up rock disturbs their nest, one hundred drill wasps descend on the group. To allay any fears, the group decides to keep score on this round of combat. Whoever gets the most wasp kills gets a reward decided upon by the players.

14 The players are passed by a loud, sputtering, fast-moving horseless carriage that is clearly out of control. After it zooms past, there is an explosion up ahead. The driver promises the players a great reward if they are willing to help take all the carriage pieces back to her workshop.

15 A crowd of people, animals, and other assorted creatures runs toward the players, then past them (in the opposite direction the group is traveling). The adventurers can see smoke in the distance and hear screams.

16 The Big Ballad Inn is the only place for miles, and they don't take coin. Patrons must sing in payment. How good they are determines what room they get.

17 In the night, a strange creature sticks out a thumb, apparently wanting a ride or traveling companions. If the group agrees, the creature follows along with the group. It helps in any combat encounter viciously and cruelly. If the group goes too long without a fight, the creature talks about eating the others. If the group refuses its company, it attacks immediately, shape-shifting into various grotesque abominations.

18 Two sets of people stand on either side of the road, arguing. They've drawn a line down the center of the road that's a hundred feet long. Someone on either side of the road says that the players better walk that line to stay neutral. Walking too close to either group will be seen as siding with that group and they will start a fight.

19 There is a traffic jam ahead. Carts are lined up in front of what appears to be a collection of boulders. A rock elemental has fallen asleep on the road. The area around the road is too rough for carriages to cross safely, but no one wants to anger the elemental by waking it.

20 Children can be seen on the side of the road playing with a big book. When the players get close enough to discern what type of book, the mood changes. The kids are playing with a deathspell tome.

21 A roadside antique store catches the players' attention. The owner here will buy anything, and there are some hidden treasures in the shop if the group is willing to spend time looking.

22 At a crossroads, the players notice a strange horned figure standing in the middle of the road. They're offering mastery of any talent, but at a cost to be collected...later.

23 The road becomes darker than the time of day should allow. It is so dark. Impossibly dark. The players are beginning to worry. They can't see anything. Torches aren't working. What is happening?

24 The weather keeps shifting from one violent extreme to another. Pouring rain, pounding snow, extreme heat, and violent winds happen at seemingly random intervals. Farther up the road, a gnome is trying to fix a strange contraption labeled "The Weather Predictor."

25 Something is wrong with the method of travel the players are using. They can keep pushing and arrive at their destination on time, but risk losing the transport, or they can work on a solution, but that may take much longer.

26 The group passes a small farm with a huge footprint in the middle of the tilled land. The farmer here is distraught. A giant's careless step means the farmer and her family may not make it through the winter. Do the players offer help?

27 The players come upon a very strange-looking town. It seems the town and everything in it have been cursed to become candy. The residents seem fine. It's a pretty normal town, if you can get past everything being made out of sugary sweets.

28 A racing stadium can be seen in the distance. There are daily races to be bet on. Anyone can enter. The prize money is a pretty large pile of gold.

29 The players encounter a small town where all disputes are solved by collectable card game matches. You need a place to stay, and the inn requires victory on the dual grid as payment.

30 Everyone realizes at nearly the same moment that they are ravenous for anything besides their packed rations.

31 A crowd has gathered to watch the Magic 5000, where competitors race with any means necessary for locomotion, but only using themselves. No vehicles, teams, or mounts. Magic is most definitely allowed.

32 A bountiful field by the road seems to be growing a multitude of delicious fruits and vegetables. In fact, if a player looks for a specific plant, it seems to present itself immediately. A simple sign reads "Only take one."

33 Not far out of town, the players encounter a child who has run away from home. The kid wants to know if they can tag along to "be a real hero like you!"

34 The smell of hundreds of flowers announces the upcoming town before anyone can see it. The townsfolk act normal, but it is clear that they are all reanimated dead.

35 The players' route coincides with a regional festival's long-distance relay race. There's a prize for the fastest group, and your party just happens to have the exact right number of people to register as a team.

36 An alarm sounds behind the players on the road. Someone in uniform steps out of the carriage and brandishes a badge. They claim to be a deputy from a nearby town, and that the group is speeding and will need to pay a hefty fine right now if they don't want trouble.

37 The most annoying bard imaginable is walking the same route as the players and will *not* take the hint that the group would rather travel alone. Couldn't she at least tune that lute? Its resonance sounds so...wrong. The players keep getting sleepier the longer she plays too. The bard offers, "Oh, I'd be ever so happy to keep watch if you need a short rest." She's using magic to put the party to sleep so she can take all their money.

38 Someone is yelling for help on the side of the road. It's actually a mimic trying to lure travelers into its trap.

39 An unassuming, short figure walks up and challenges the players to a race. If the players win, they get a sack of coins, but if the stranger wins, the players must do them "just a little favor."

40 Small, adorable creatures are curious about the players. They are soft, furry, and sweet. They seem malnourished but are happy enough to eat any food the players offer. They reproduce quickly, and eventually turn into gigantic furry monsters that will eat *anything*.

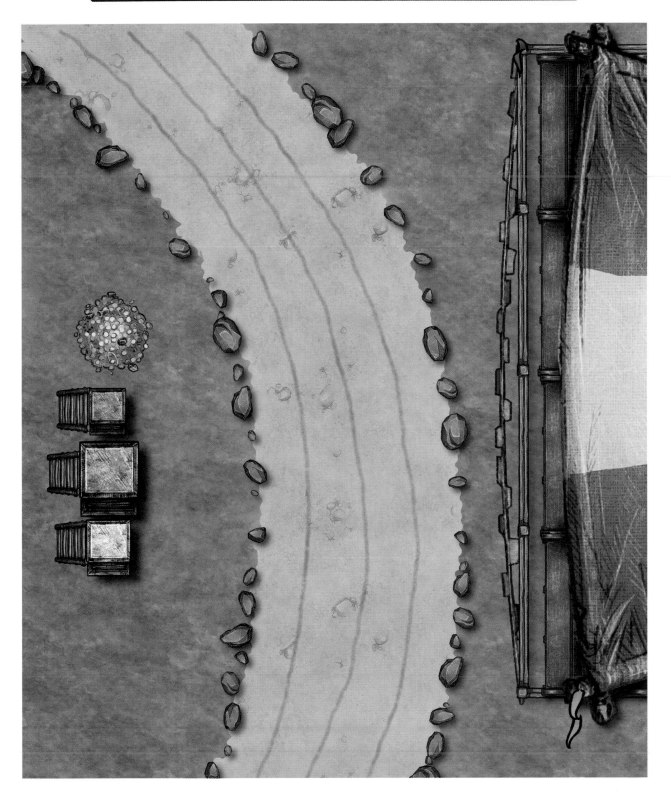

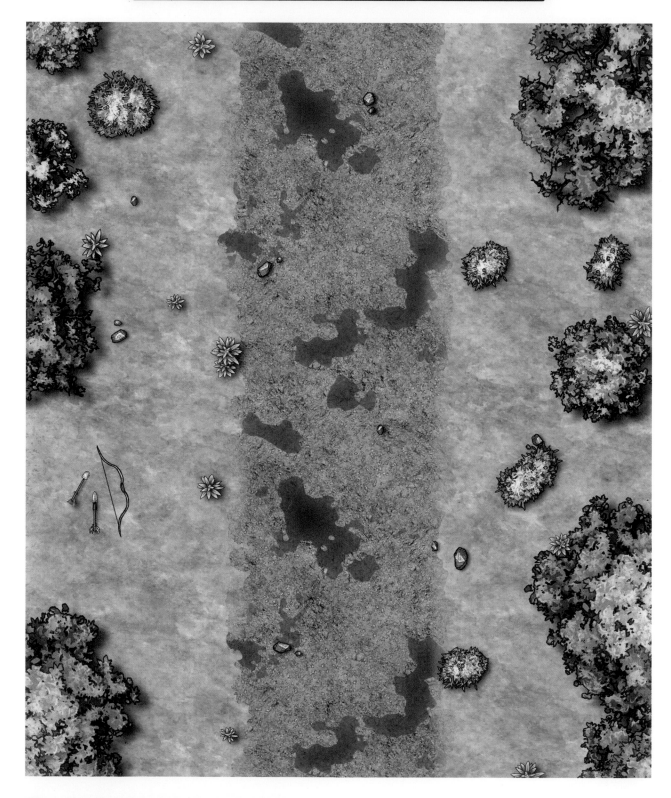

41 An arrow whizzes by one of the character's heads. You glimpse a figure ducking behind cover in the distance. It looks like someone has it out for the group!

42 A wizard and his two companions stop the party as they approach. He states that the road ahead has been blocked by an unforeseen disaster and he is willing to teleport them well past the danger; he will do anything to convince the party to take this offer. If the players refuse, he will attack.

43 Howls can be heard in the distance. A werewolf pack seems to be tracking the players down the road, getting closer and closer.

44 A group of masked bandits circles the players on the road, intent on taking all the wealth they can. They are led by a towering figure with long horns.

45 The group has run into a muddy patch. Their journey will take significantly longer if they can't come up with a way to clear this terrain quickly.

46 A large deer appears and seems to beckon to the group to follow it. If they hunt the deer, it will grow larger and attack back. If they follow it, it will lead them to a small clearing where the god of the forest bestows a blessing upon them.

47 A huge fog bank rolls in out of nowhere. Inside of it, compasses don't work, and the players are worried they may get turned around. That's when the growling starts. Incredibly close, and immediately threatening.

48 Everyone is bored with the slowness of their travel. What ideas does the group have for increasing their travel speed?

49 The heavy rain has washed away the mud that was covering a small hole beneath a tree next to the road. Hidden inside the hole is a waterproof scroll case that contains the last will and testament of Gayatri Ner and the deed to a town called Neverwind. It seems that Gayatri wanted his daughter Phaenna to have it all.

50 Ear-piercing squealing can be heard from nearby bushes before a horde of bear boars tumbles out, running at full speed directly toward the players.

51 The players find themselves in an area completely unfamiliar to them. They can double back and find their way again, adding a bunch of extra time to their journey, or they can try to find some directions here.

52 The players are being followed. Someone is hiding *almost* well enough to go undetected, but several signs eventually discovered by the characters make it clear someone is in pursuit.

53 A creepy scarecrow in the field to the right catches everyone's attention. It keeps appearing in fields as the players travel. It seems a little closer to the road every time anyone sees it.

54 Rain has been drenching the land (and the players) for miles. The road is completely mud, greatly impairing progress. As the group slogs through, strange shapes begin emerging from the ground. Mud fiends are attacking!

55 The group gradually becomes aware of a strange figure following them at a slow pace. Each time they look back, the figure is a bit closer. As it gets nearer, each character sees the figure as a different person from their past. It's coming closer.

56 Along the side of the road, someone has set up a large food cart and places to sit. A good number of travelers are there eating, including a few who say they've come from faraway towns. The food is good, but rumors and information are also on the menu here.

57 The group comes upon a bunch of merchants. What they are selling looks like it may have been stolen from the village the players stayed in two nights before.

58 A procession is filling up most of the road. Holy knights on horses are surrounding what looks to be a young man being forced to walk while the others ride. The young man is on a pilgrimage, and the only food he is allowed to have must be given freely by those he meets and will take pity on him. His feet look sore and raw but he seems in good spirits. If the party parts with some food, the young man blesses them with good luck lasting three days.

59 A traveling merchant sits by the side of the road with many interesting items for sale but is very keen on selling an amulet to the players, promising it has magic. The merchant has trapped the spirit of a rival in the amulet and wants the item far away from here so it can't be found and reunited with the rival's body.

60 The group passes a wagon that appears stopped but is actually moving in slow motion. If the group can dispel the time magic, the driver introduces themself as the Wodgian Wizard of the Wend. The wizard offers a card with their picture on it. This spell card can force an object to move in slow motion for ten minutes.

61 A caravan of wagons by the side of the road has decided to show their animals. Many are common animals that are dressed up to be something more monstrous, like a dog with a bunch of tentacles attached to a sweater. However, the final wagon does have something truly monstrous, a hydra that hisses and snaps at anyone who hangs around too long.

62 Up ahead an ornate carriage is stopped on the side of the road and two men can be heard arguing. They introduce themselves as Gavin and Niall, recently just married. However, their map is malfunctioning. Anyone who looks at the map sees something different. The men are willing to give up the map for one that is more reliable.

63 A traveling carnival caravan sits by the side of the road with a broken carriage wheel. They call out to the passing players for help. Keen-eyed players notice everyone seems to be concealing a weapon. An obvious trap. Maybe it's still worth the tussle to free the carnival beasts?

64 The sign outside of this odd roadside caravan reads "Shady Quinn School of Hard Knocks." A sketchy-looking man calling himself Shady Quinn says that his expert professors in the arts of combat and magic await. For 5 gold, the players can test their skills against one of the professors. Win, and the professor gives them a magic item appropriate to the skill or attribute they were testing.

65 A gnome in a strange carriage powered by magic pulls up to the players and offers a ride to wherever they're going. If the players accept the ride, the doors of the carriage lock and the gnome takes off at breakneck speed, but not to the destination they wanted to go.

66 A sign shaped like a gigantic sword points to the left fork in the road leading to "Big Sal's BIG WEAPONS," a shop selling an arsenal of oversized weapons that are light as a feather. Big Sal offers to let the group "try before they buy" by fighting him in a duel.

67 The only tavern for miles is The Pure Soul tavern. There are alcoves where one can think upon their misdeeds, and they only serve dry bread and water. In order to stay, one must truthfully confess their best and worst deed.

68 The road splits here, with one path leading down into a ravine, and the other path being the high road that follows the lip of the ravine. Those that take the low road are accosted by large worms. Taking the high road subjects the players to attack by giant birds.

69 A huge arrow sign on the road reads "Unlimited danger! Test your might! Fight our best!" It's basically a gym with competition and training in mind.

70 Something sticking out of the ground catches the players' eyes. At the same moment, another group of folks on the road sees the same thing. The chest contains an obscene amount of gold. The other group says they saw it first.

71 An obviously false facade of a building proclaims "sOrds aNd kuL Stuf." It's a pop-up shop run by a short goblin entrepreneur. The items are quite aggressively priced, but the blood and gore still remaining on the equipment suggests the goblin dragged these out of a dungeon after another adventuring party failed their quest.

72 A rockier, smaller path diverts from the road ahead. The path is littered with warning signs about bandits, monsters, and pitfalls. There is also a destination sign letting the players know the place they are headed can be reached *much* more quickly by taking this path.

73 "Madame Wizzo's Cirque du Cirque—Happiest Place in the Realm" proclaims the enormous sign decorating a defunct fairground to the left of the path. If the players venture in, undead clowns with their equally undead trained animal companions attack!

74 A messenger galloping at top speed catches up to the players and delivers a message. An emergency has arisen where the players had headed from, and their presence is requested. Of course, this will be a long detour, but the message sounds fairly desperate.

75 "World's Scariest Haunted House" signs have been placed on the roadside. If the group dares to venture to this destination, they find a deserted shack with a slot inside labeled "1 gold." If they insert a gold coin, a trap door opens, releasing dozens of very real zombies.

76 Another group of adventurers passes by going the other way. The group wants to share stories but is collectively very competitive. If they are begrudgingly impressed by the players' tales, they offer to spar with the group.

77 A sign proclaims "World's Largest Bone Slug, Next Right!" If the players decide to go see it, they find the bone slug running rampant, attempting to eat all the tourists!

78 This roadside inn and tavern is called L'Idée Déjouée and seems to be a large wooden horse that has been converted into two tap rooms, one room in each leg, and a bunch of bedrooms in the upper levels. Between the two legs is an open beer garden and travelers seem to be having a wonderful time.

79 Ahead in the road, a huge herd of venom sheep is crossing the road. They completely block the way.

80 The stars the players have been using to navigate are suddenly in different locations in the sky. The road doesn't seem to have changed direction, but the party is now worried they may be going in the wrong direction. How will they get back on track?

81 Ahead, the party can see a huge globe floating above the horizon. As they get nearer, they begin traveling underneath it. The players can feel a competing gravity tug at them, like if they jumped high enough, they could fall up to this huge place. Looking at the globe, the players see a similar landscape to their current surroundings.

82 There is a crash, sending everyone toppling to the ground. Have everyone describe an injury they got in the spill. What kind of first aid is needed? Do they get that right away?

83 The players accidentally make a turn into the middle of a parade. Do they try to blend in? Do they have any trinkets to throw to the crowd? Do they know what the parade is for? What *is* it for?

84 A young person approaches the players, explaining that they are an actor (currently uncast, but they *will* be a star). They'd like to tag along on any adventures you might be having as a method acting study.

85 A small shrine is set up alongside the road. Inside the shrine are twelve scrolls and a small sign that says "Take a scroll, leave a scroll." There is a one in one hundred chance that some kind person left an actual magic spell scroll. Mostly it's odd bits of news and fiction stories.

86 Some children are skipping in a circle chanting, "Let's all die! Let's all die!" When the kids notice the players, they stop suddenly and begin skipping toward the players. As they get closer, the players can see that these children are pale, almost pale green, and their flesh is rotten.

87 Hastily thrown up fences on the roadside are ominous warnings that something needs to be kept out. Wheezing, scratching, and gurgling noises in the shadows keep the players on edge.

88 This area appears to be a war zone. The players can try to traverse, but they may become entangled in this conflict. There are also areas with magical mines buried in the ground.

89 Just ahead the players can see the wreckage site of many crashed wagons. It looks like some impromptu battle happened here, and that both parties may have wiped each other out.

90 A bunch of fairies and pixies have set up a yard sale. They are selling normal things like pine cones, acorns, and leaves, but they also have a few items and potions that only can come from the fairy realms. The prices vary greatly, from simple gold for the acorns, to more esoteric asks like three hairs from a person's head, or a bag full of a person's breath.

91 The main bridge on this road is suddenly a toll bridge by order of the governor. Traffic has backed up, as people weren't expecting to have to pay, merchants are complaining, and more than a few people can't pay the toll. Soldiers are telling people if they can't pay, they can take a loan from the governor and pay it back in a week's time.

92 Blissfully, someone has set up a couple of nice outhouses and a table and bench off to the side of the road. A few people have carved sayings and crude drawings on the top of the table; the most notable drawing seems to be of a treasure map leading farther off the road from here.

93 After a long day, the only place to stop is the Cutthroat Inn. A sign on the door says "Enter at your own risk," and the clientele looks very dangerous. Pickpockets constantly roam the main room and literally everyone is spoiling for a fight, especially the waitstaff and the barkeep.

94 A section of the road is suddenly washed out, and the bridge is gone as well. Water keeps swelling up in the area. A bit farther downstream, the players find a dire beaver who has made a dam and used the old bridge as part of it. The beaver looks menacing.

95 This village is home to a retired wizard who is spending their twilight years making fun toys and games. The characters have a lively day helping the wizard think of increasingly elaborate games for the kids of the village. Weeks later, they get a letter from the wizard saying that one of the games they invented really took off. Enclosed is the recipe for a potent healing potion as a way of saying thanks.

96 The Intrigue Tavern is famous along this road and is an excellent source of information and, well, intrigue. A sign on the door states the simple rules: One, everyone must wear a mask. Two, no real names can be used. Three, everyone must buy a drink and dinner to stay at the tavern all night. If anyone breaks the rules, they are forever banned from the place. But there is a great amount of information to be gathered here.

97 This patch of the road is suddenly slick with ice and is almost impossible to walk or stand on. A white-robed wizard steps out from a hiding place, cackling and shouting, "At last I have you! My revenge is near!" One of the player's ancestors cheated this very wizard, and he's out for blood.

98 Piles of rock make this section of the road difficult to travel upon. Closer inspection of the rocks reveals that they were once part of a statue and could be put back together with just a little hard work. If anyone puts the statue back together, it comes to life and immediately attacks the group.

99 A group of the king's soldiers blocks the path ahead; however, they have turned to banditry due to a recent coup in the kingdom. A player recognizes one of the bandits, and there is an opportunity to avoid conflict here, but they want the players to get involved with taking their kingdom back.

100 A large sleeping beast is lying across the road and blocking everyone's way. No attempt to wake it has been successful. It's possible that a bard will remember a tale about a special song played on a flute that will wake this creature. If they do so, the beast awakens, is angry, and attacks.

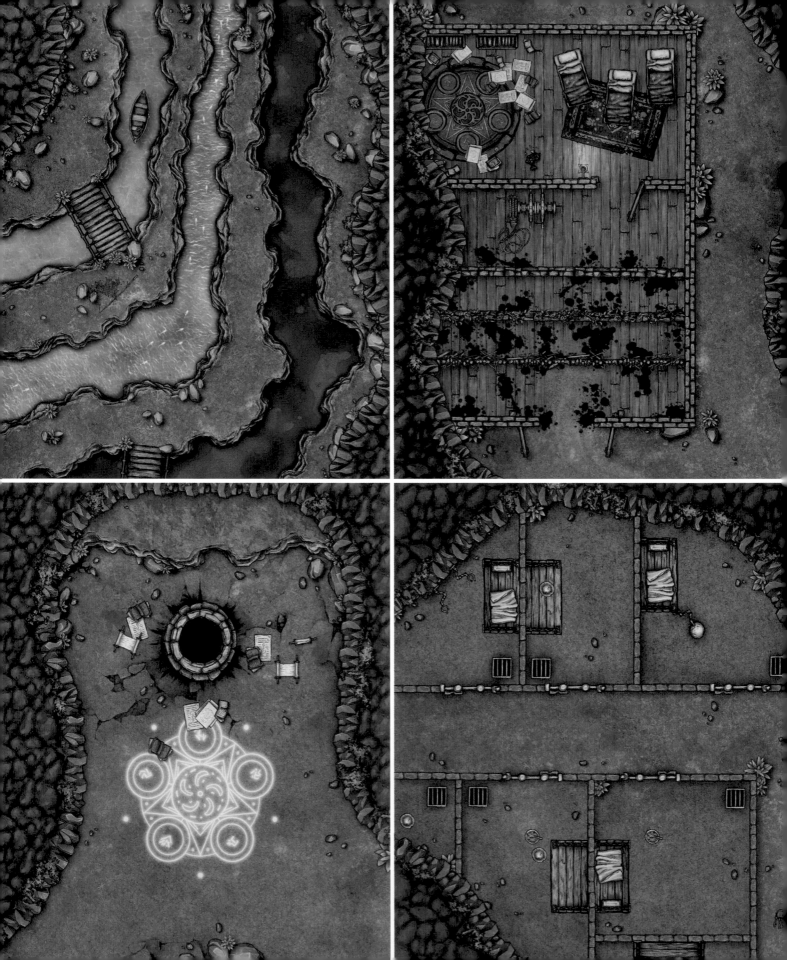

DUNGEON

Running a dungeon session often feels like a completely different task than sessions set elsewhere. Most of the time you're running an RPG, you're not concerned with every little step the characters take. You narrate a bit, do a montage here or there, and then "zoom in" once you've gotten the party to the next encounter. In a dungeon though, the party is likely expecting danger at any corner, so you wind up "zoomed in" much more often. Something as simple as opening a door could take multiple steps if a player is concerned the door is trapped or wants to get an idea of what's behind it before passing through. As a result, a good number of the encounters on this list are contained within one room. If your party is crawling through a dungeon, these provide a perfect way to populate each with fun things to do. Other entries on the list describe an encounter that encompasses an entire dungeon, which is helpful if you are looking for a quicker delve. In either case, if you're rolling on these tables randomly, it would behoove you to decide if the encounter you land on is the type you're looking for. As always, feel free to cheat and roll again until you get one that fits what you need. In general, expect traps, fights, and escapes!

1   A series of blades on pendulums swings through this room, making a path to the far door difficult. All the pendulums after the first two are illusions, but so is the floor, and anyone who doesn't notice is dropped onto spikes.

2   The player walking at the front of the group is suddenly caught in a web. Hisses can be heard as several giant spiders lower from the ceiling.

3   The character at the front suddenly runs into a wall. The players find themselves surrounded by mirrors. A figure in a lumpy red cloak appears in each mirror. It's the Wodgian Wizard of the Wiles. If the players can escape the mirror trap, the wizard offers a card with their picture on it. This spell card can be used to trap a target in a mirror maze.

4   An imposing minotaur sits at the entrance of this room. He tells the players there is no other way through except to enter his maze competition.

5   There are as many mirrors on the east wall as there are party members. When someone stands in front of a mirror, a skeleton appears to them in the mirror. The skeleton then leaps from the mirror and attacks.

6   The players are headed down a hallway when they hear a click. Suddenly a huge boulder is rumbling toward them!

7   The players enter a new chamber styled like a living room. There's a fireplace, comfy chairs, and above the mantel, there's a portrait...of one of the players. When that character sees the portrait, they are instantly teleported inside of it and a doppelganger version of them attacks the rest of the players.

8   Every surface in this room is a mirror. There are many cliffs and pillars making the room feel odd. Upon entering, the players see their reflections run off, and they must catch them in order to get out of this now-sealed room.

9   This room is a giant balance scale. Upon entry, the door slams shut and this section of the room begins to move. If the players did mostly good deeds, the floor will raise, and the other side will lower. Demons will appear and attack them. If they did bad deeds, the floor lowers and angels appear on the other side of the room and attack.

10 The floor in this room is full of sand that is extremely hard to walk through. There is a hole in the arched ceiling just big enough for someone to fit through. Once everyone is in the room, the door locks tight behind them and the room turns upside down. The sand covers everyone as it begins to pour through the hole. Once all the sand has run through the hole, the next door will open.

11 A statue of a horse has a sign nearby that says "Do Not Ride the Horse." Anyone close to the horse feels magically compelled to get in the saddle. If anyone does, the horse animates and charges away from the rest of the group.

12 A small dragon-like creature pops its head out from the ceiling and asks how the players are liking things so far. The creature is really just trying to scope out how strong the players are in order to devise better traps for farther in.

13 The floor in this room is jelly and hard to walk across but is otherwise harmless.

14 This large room seems to be a chapel. Farther back in the room, you can see a large scaffold suspended from the ceiling by ropes. Monstrous humming can be heard from the creature or creatures that are on the scaffold painting the wall.

15 Opening the door to this room causes a key to slowly lower down from the ceiling, toward a large vat of acid. If the door is opened all the way or carelessly, the key is dumped and dissolved by the acid pool.

16 This long room is divided by a large pool of water that is 50 feet across. Within the pool are intelligent sharks that are all equipped with wands that can shoot missiles of magic at anyone who tries to cross the water.

17 This room has thick wall-to-wall carpeting. Once anyone reaches the middle of the room, they start sinking into the ground, and any attempt at using the walls or ceiling has the same result.

18 This 10' × 10' room is covered floor to ceiling with nearly translucent eggs. A small path leads through the room to the door on the other side. One touch to an egg causes it to spray acid, leading to a chain reaction in which all the eggs explode.

19 Inside this room is a chicken in front of a chessboard. A sign reads "Defeat me and get a great reward." If the players beat the chicken, it lays a ruby egg. If they lose, goblins rush out and attack them.

20 This room has a jumble of red and blue lines that cross the entire floor. They can be carefully avoided, but touching a red line causes the room to become damagingly hot, and touching a blue line causes it to become damagingly cold.

21 The walls of the room pulse with the movement of many spiders. Upon closer inspection, the creatures aren't spiders but many disembodied hands that leap off the walls and try to grab anything they can easily steal.

22 No sound comes from behind the locked door to this room. When the door is opened, obnoxious singing escapes the once-soundproof room. In the center of the room is a singing sword chained to the ground; it begs to be freed with a song.

23 The players find a grungy general store. Most of the items are things people have dropped and odd bits of food. However, there are a couple of potions that look like they are magical and might heal the party. In the second room, there is a goblin priest who is able to make potions but very slowly, as they don't have access to good supplies.

24 In this dungeon, a makeshift stage and audience seating are set up. It looks like the dungeon's denizens are rehearsing for a play with pyrotechnics and wire-flying rigs. Do the players attack underworld villains or take part in a momentary bit of fun with bizarre dungeon dwellers?

25 Suits of armor line the walls of this room. The players need to avoid stepping on the brightly colored tiles in the room, or they will spring a trap where the suits of armor unsheathe their weapons and steadily walk toward the center of the room to cut anyone in their way.

26 This room has a tiny model of the full dungeon set up in the middle of the room with small effigies of each character. The group notices a small mass of tentacled shadows slowly making its way toward the room their effigies are in.

27 A river winds through this room. The players hear chattering and laughing coming out of the tunnel to the north. A small, round boat floats out of the north wall with a party of goblins chatting to each other inside. If the players attack, the goblins fight back. Riding the boat or swimming in the river leads to a large room where a new set of goblins climbs into the boat for their ride. Hundreds of goblins are waiting in line.

28 The upper part of this room is filled with gas. Any open flame will cause it to explode.

29 The floor suddenly gives out and those that fall are dropped into a boat on a raging river. Falling debris damages the hull of the boat and cuts the rope holding the boat in place. The players must navigate the fast-moving river, patch the holes, and remove the extra weight in the boat to get to a safe embankment.

30 The floor in this room is lava, but there is a strange-looking bridge leading across the room. When the players are halfway across, the bridge begins to shake. Turns out, the bridge is a giant, many-legged lavapede!

31 The floor is pulsing with the bodies of millions of cockroaches.

32 A fast-moving river flows through this room, entering the room on the north side and exiting the room on the west side. The current is very strong and large, white, glowing fish can be seen swimming against the current within the river. On the opposite bank, a group of monsters is fishing out of the river and attacks anyone who tries to poach their fishing spot.

33 A troll demands payment to cross a narrow bridge over a very deep chasm. If paid, the troll speaks a word, and the illusory bridge becomes real. If the players refuse or kill the troll, the bridge fades from view.

34 The stench of sulfur is powerful here. A fetid, yellowish-green pool lines the far wall. While the room initially looks like a dead end, the next room can be reached by diving through the pool. Any who dare to do this emerge extremely stinky but otherwise unharmed.

35 The players run into a young adventurer running the opposite direction. They are bloody and terrified. They ask for help and offer warnings of something *big* heading this way.

36 A river flows through this room from north to west, but the water is definitely not normal. It is blood red and reeks of death and decay. Anyone approaching the river needs a strong constitution or will lose their lunch at the sight and smell. Those foolish enough to follow the river to the north will come upon a vomitorium and into a large slaughterhouse.

37 When the players enter this room, select a party member to recall a memory where they were in danger. This room becomes that situation, but whatever solution they used to get out of this in the past no longer works.

38 The gravity in this room increases the farther one walks in, threatening to crush anyone by the time they get to the door. The only way through is to find a way to reach a lever near the ceiling... halfway into the room.

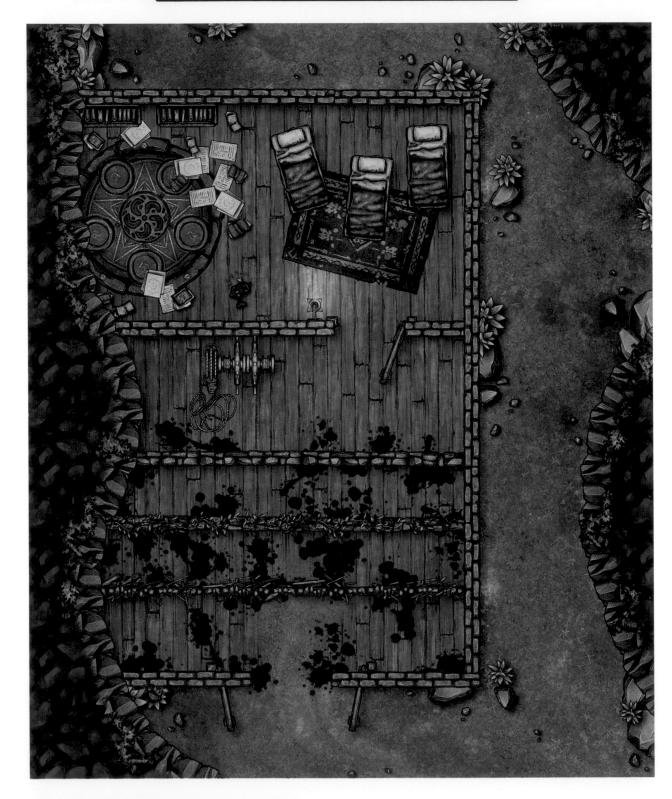

39 Goblins are living in the next two rooms. In the first, they have created three barricades to hide behind and have covered the floor in a tarry substance to slow anyone down. They also have built a pulley system into the ceiling to escape upward if they need to. Many goblins guard this post to protect the homes they have made in the second room.

40 As the floor depresses, walls slam up, separating each hero in their own locked room. Each player must face off against their own monster without the help of the others. Once a monster is defeated, one of the separating walls drops, letting that hero help another.

41 The players have reached a goblin lair. Ten goblins stand behind three imposing structures that are covered with religious iconography of their god. The scenes all seem to depict the goblin god crushing human villages. The goblins attempt to convert the players to the goblins' human-crushing religion. They don't see any reason why humans can't join as long as they like to crush other humans.

42 This exceptionally large room is bright and sunny, with a large fake sun near the ceiling. Large trees and flowing grasses make this room feel like a nice, quiet park. Anyone can stay here undisturbed for as long as they want.

43 A small band of about fifteen dwarves is holding this room. They state that they have cleared everything up through this room and that it's unsafe for anyone to continue past them until they've rested. They don't want anyone else moving forward either, as they have claimed this dungeon as theirs.

44 A sign on the door says "Don't Wake Mommy." Inside the room is a giant bedroom with a sleeping dragon on the bed. There are treasures everywhere, but anything too loud, including opening the door, will wake the dragon and she will attack.

45 Goblins have taken over these next two rooms. A single goblin greets the party at the door; it speaks goblin but can understand a common language. In the room, there are three walls built. One is made of random sticks held together with small bits of mud. The second wall is made of still wet and oozing mud, and the third is built of stone. The goblin at the door asks the players to try to destroy each wall while the goblin's clan watches.

46 This room is filled with trash. There are definitely treasures to be found in the piles, but 90 percent of the objects have been dumped in here because they are cursed.

47 There is a coffin in the center of the room. If anyone knocks or jostles the coffin, a voice inside says, "Just five more minutes, please." If they open the coffin, a very angry vampire attacks the players.

48 Strange clocks are set on shelves and pedestals around the room. Each clock is running fast or slow. Anyone who touches a clock is jumped back or forward according to the time listed on the clock.

49 This dungeon turns out to be the well-camouflaged rear entrance to an organized crime hideout.

50 A 5- by 5-foot room has shelves on three walls filled with goblets of all sizes and styles. A ghost appears briefly and says, "Choose carefully."

51 As the players enter this room, the floor sinks a bit and all the doors slam closed. At the top of a 30-foot-tall ceiling, a candle can be seen burning through a rope connecting to the structure the players are standing on. If burned through, the floor will fall to unknown depths!

52 On the west side of the wall is a series of holes and on the east side of the room is a series of globes that are the same size as the holes. Touching a globe causes it to shoot violently across into the hole on the opposite side. Most will explode and let out poisonous gas, but players can see a lever in one of the holes that will unlock the door on the south end of the room. The lever can only be moved when the right globe hits it.

53 Once all the players have entered this room, they lose a body part. It's painless and they can no longer feel that limb. A chamber at the far end opens, and a strange creature attacks using their missing limbs. They will get their limbs back if they can defeat the creature without hurting their own missing limbs.

54 The players interrupt a summoning ritual being performed by a cult. The intrusion apparently makes the summoning misfire, and an incorrect (and very deadly) monster is drawn through the portal.

55 A very powerful sword sits in a glass case in the center of this room. A sign reads "State a time in the future, and I will be with you for the duration." If they say a minute, the sword will appear in a minute and last a minute. If they say a year, the sword will appear to them in a year and last for a year.

56 A large room has an open pit in the center. At the bottom of the pit one can see many doors, but there is also a giant centipede.

57 This small room smells terrible. There is a hole in the ground that is completely dark. Next to the hole are a few pages from a book or a scroll of some kind. As you examine the room, a large troll rushes up behind you, clearly in a hurry.

58 A magic cauldron draws all metal objects to it as soon as anyone enters the room. If anything is successfully drawn to the cauldron, it magically lifts into the air and flies out of the room and away from the players.

59 A strange beam of light strikes the first person who enters this room, followed by a weird noise. In the center of the room, the players see an automaton being magically built from the floor up; it's a replica of the light-struck person.

60 At the far end of this dead-end room is a raised rock platform about 4 feet off the ground. As the players enter, human-sized puppets drop from the ceiling and start acting out everything the players have done in the dungeon so far.

61 A bubbling cauldron sits in the center of the room. As the players enter, it begins to bubble over and ooze out of the sides. The ooze animates and begins to attack the players with its pseudopods.

62 In the center of the room is a pedestal with a book on it and in the book is a handwritten list of places. If anyone writes a place in the book, a portal appears linked to that place. It's a one-way trip.

63 As the players enter, scraping can be heard on the other side of this long hall. The stone-slab door at the end of the hall is gradually lowering. Between the players and that door, there are a dozen or so angry demons clearly looking to slow them down.

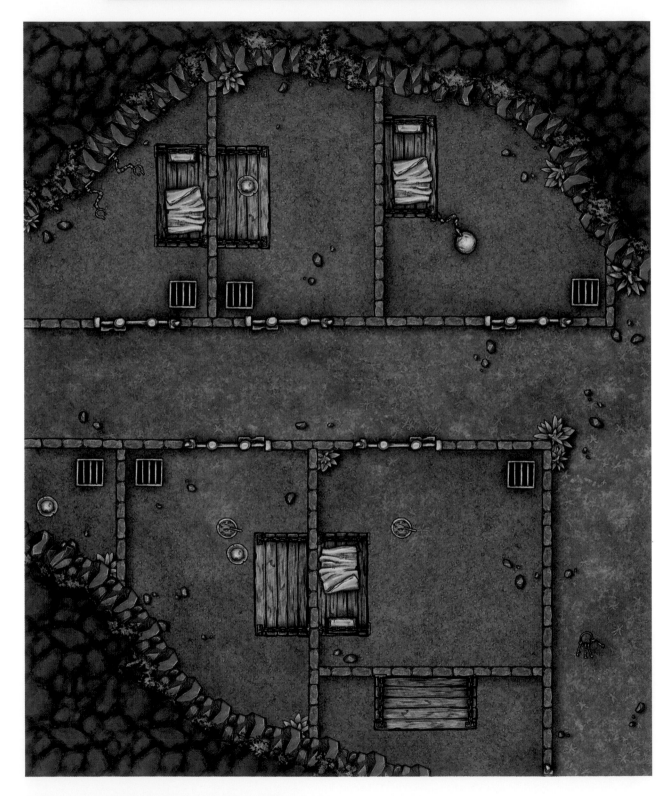

64 In this room is a series of small doors. There is one small door on the floor, one small door on the ceiling, one small door on the west wall, and one small door on the east wall. On the north wall, there are two small doors, one marked with the letter A and the other marked with the letter B. In the center of the room is a marker with a pair of shoes facing north. If the players open the ceiling door twice, the floor door twice, then the left door, right door, left door, right door, and then the B door, and finally the A door, a diamond worth 10,000 gold appears in the room. If they do this out of order, they must leave the room to reset it. Any wrong order also makes a monster appear in the room and attack them.

65 Five elves guard what is clearly just an adventuring party. The elves ask if the players are the legal counsel requested for these criminals. If not, the elves attempt to throw the players in prison as well!

66 A series of twisting lines is painted on the wall. On the side by the door they just entered is the painting of a key with a colored lined leaving from it leading to the other door, which is locked. The center of the room is blank and there are pots of paint matching all the colors of the lines on a shelf nearby. Painting in the correct line will open the door. Each incorrect line causes a monster to manifest into the room.

67 This 40- by 40-foot room is clearly some sort of cafeteria. Many of the monsters and guards are sitting at tables, obviously in self-selected groups. The smell of food is odd but still enticing. It's well lit; there are some tables and chairs, and some bags of food with phrases like "Gronk's fud, NO eat!"

68 A villain is trapped in this dungeon against their will. They offer a temporary truce if the players will help them escape.

69 At the far end of the room is a statue of a woman with a very expensive ring on her finger. If the ring is removed, a banshee appears and attacks the players until the ring is placed back on the statue's finger.

70 This chamber looks like a courtroom. The goblin seated at the enormous stone judge's bench points an accusing finger at the players and says, "You have been charged with trespassing, reckless endangerment, and murder! How do you plead?"

71 A gnome bursts through the wall riding some sort of mechanized drill. He says he got tired of the maze and just started going wherever he wanted on his new invention. He'll gladly let anyone walk through his tunnels.

72 The players come across another set of adventurers who have been lost in this dungeon for weeks. They beg the players to help them find the way out. If the players refuse, or put the adventurers in danger, they will attack and try to steal anything that may help them get out or survive.

73 Four locked doors line the west wall of this hallway. There is a person behind each door who promises something valuable in return for being set free. Three of the prisoners are monsters in disguise who will attack the players if set free. One prisoner can actually grant the players a boon if set free.

74 The players have been thrown in the dungeon for crimes against the kingdom, but they have proof that the king is a demon in disguise. No one has ever escaped these dungeons...yet.

75 The floor in the center of the room is broken, almost like a crater. Each hour, a huge boulder is dropped from the high ceiling, then hauled back to the top on a chain.

76 The eastern wall here has four different glyphs made of emerald, ruby, sapphire, and topaz. The group will have to play a memory game where a pattern lights up on the glyphs, then that same pattern needs to be touched, in order, by the players. The pattern gets longer and faster as they progress.

77 This room has sets of stairs set randomly in the room, attached to the ceiling, walls, and floor in weird orientations. The gravity is specific to each set of stairs so that they can always be used properly, but moving from each set of stairs is very disorienting and requires challenging feats of athleticism.

78 This room is a dance hall with specters offering their hands to the players. If the players choose to dance, they'll need to be good enough not to ruin the party.

79 A large wooden rod stands in the center of this room. There are no other doors. Anyone who is strong enough to twist the stick finds that they are actually turning the whole room, aligning the door they came in through with new doors as the room turns.

80 The players move on to the next door and find themselves in a room they've seen before. This dungeon's chambers can shift and relocate.

81 This room is an ancient, long-forgotten library. The books and scrolls are well preserved but in ancient versions of modern languages.

82 Opening the door lights a fuse to a large bomb at the other side of the room. Those fast enough and strong enough might be able to break the fuse before the big explosion.

83 A pile of rats in a trench coat sits in a small shop stall setup. The rats have some cheese (bitten), decaying bodies ("delicious," according to the sign), and precious gemstones ("yucky tasting") for sale. The only currency they recognize is food.

84 The steps of this staircase are marked with a repeating pattern, one letter per step going up: "C D E F G A B C." Next to the stairs on the wall is a complicated tune that shows which steps are safe to use.

85 The chest in the center of the room is a creature mimicking being a chest for fun. Opening the chest causes the chest to scream and bare its teeth for a moment, then laugh. It can only speak its own language but can tell the party where it hid the real chest full of gold and jewels.

86 Upon entering the room, everyone's memories are wiped clean. Within the first minute everyone can remember how to speak and talk to each other but nothing about who they are or why they are here. Players need to ask each other questions and state enough facts about each other that their characters can fill in their own memories.

87 This room is a series of ramps and half-pipes. A goblin on a skateboard hands the players a skateboard and challenges them to beat his style.

88 This room is clearly an infirmary. Hurt dungeon denizens can be found healing in here.

89 This well-lit chamber is completely empty. As the last person enters, the door slams shut, plunging everyone in darkness. Small balls of light appear and swirl around the players before giggling and fleeing into various parts of the chamber. Light magic will not work here. The players must lure or convince the fae lights to help them escape the treacherous pathway that leads out of this room.

90 This room has stairs leading up to what seems to be the next level of the room. Anyone who reaches the fifth step causes all the stairs to slam down, creating a ramp that acts like a belt pulling the players quickly up the ramp at a terrifying speed. Anyone who isn't quick or nimble enough is launched off the top of the ramp and into a deep pit. Those that can keep their footing and ride this ramp can jump off to the side in the upper room and get out safely.

91 The spiderweb above the door reads "All are welcome here." The door itself is also covered in spiderwebs. Opening the door, the players find a room covered in webs and a half-man, half-spider creature walking around on the webs. The creature smiles at the group and welcomes them in. Moving around the room is terrible because of the webs, but the creature is true to its word and doesn't attack. It will answer any questions it can but is way more interested in talking about philosophy. Scattered about the room are various items that are clearly from previous adventuring parties. The creature says it also runs a lost and found.

92 Jellyfish float in the air in this large room. Touching any of the tendrils will cause paralysis.

93 A sign on this door says "No Secrets Inside." If anyone enters, the room will attempt to read their deepest thoughts and secrets. A giant magical mouth will then say them out loud.

94 The floor in this room is wall-to-wall trampolines. Acrobatic adversaries in this room effortlessly jump from corner to corner.

95 Walking through this hallway showers the players with sneezing powder. Those of weak constitution will sneeze loudly for the next two hours.

96 This room is filled with fine cheeses. Anyone who lingers too long will meet the giant cheesemaker, who isn't happy with visitors.

97 This is the armory. Two impressive suits of armor protect the items inside unless the passcode is given for them to stand down.

98 A series of twenty owl statues lines both the east and west walls of the room, ten on each side, and the only other exit is at the north end of this 100-foot-long and 20-foot-wide room. Three random owl eyes light up and shoot fire across the room. On each player's turn, roll a 20-sided die to determine which three statues light up and shoot fire.

99 Entering into this dark room causes the room to erupt with screams of "Surprise!" The players are showered with confetti and glitter.

100 This large room is water from top to bottom. Some sort of magic keeps it from pouring out of the door as it opens. The room is too dark to see anything much past the door.

SEA

Set sail on the sea, adventurers! The sea affords you encounter opportunities not possible elsewhere. Narrow escapes from massive sea creatures, ship-to-ship combat, and stealth boarding parties all make for uniquely fun role-playing experiences, but GMing those adventures can feel daunting once you remember just how little you know about how boats work.

Instead of fretting over details about what ropes the party needs to pull to make the sails do this or that, try assigning abstracted roles to the players. In a confrontation with another ship, one of you might be in charge of the boat's movement, another one of you controls the ship's offenses, and still another is responsible for the boarding party.

That's just one option, and the RPG system you're playing with might even have its own list of rules for how to do that. Either way, zooming out like that can be key to making sure the players feel like their actions impact the drama of the scene, not just the relative position of the rudder.

1 The players encounter a whirlpool. Investigating, they find the source is an enchanted clam pochette. The players discover they can enter the bag. Inside, they find a strange dungeon. If they can make it to the center of this dungeon maze and repair the hole in the bottom of the bag, this enchanted item will be theirs!

2 Off in the distance, the players can see a small island with an enormous pine tree growing in the dead center. The pine tree has produced a single golden pine cone at the very top of the tree. If they climb the tree, they will encounter Beetivarious the Squirrel, who will challenge the players to see if they are worthy of the acorn. She is a high-level monk and has many secret techniques to keep the pine cone safe.

3 A large crate is found floating next to the boat one morning with writing in a code or language no one knows. Inside the crate, the players find a beautiful golden urn. That night, the spirit of a sea hag that had been trapped inside the urn attempts to possess a crew member.

4 Enormous jellyfish float to the surface of the water all around the boat and then begin to float out of the water and into the sky. Their dangling tendrils are poisonous and will poison anyone unlucky enough to be struck by them.

5 The blazing sun has been bright for almost a week now and the wind has completely died. Eventually, the sun makes it too bright to stand on deck without feeling like you are burning.

6 A giant, low *flooomp* can be heard beneath the waves, then a large whirlpool forms. It seems a plug at the bottom of the ocean has become dislodged and is now vacuuming up everything in the ocean to places unknown.

7 A party of elves approaches the ship on the back of a large manta ray. They inform the players that the ship has entered their territory and they must pay a toll to cross these waters safely.

8 Strange bugs made out of water begin to swarm the ship, crawling up the sides and onto the deck. They begin to chew away at the wood and re-form back into shape if swatted into pieces.

9 Several octopuses climb into the ship. They offer a note of explanation. They are traveling salesfolk selling immaculate, magically powerful gloves (eight gloves, each with one finger per set).

10 One morning, the ship is surrounded by dead sea life. Investigation reveals that their lives were drained through some strange necrotic power under the sea.

11 A strange ziggurat is jutting impossibly out of the sea clearly anchored in place. The inside of the temple makes no sense. Hallways just end in walls, or drop-offs, stairways move as they are being used. Odd, disturbing patterns start glowing on the walls, and faint whispering can be heard. At the center of the temple is a chain box with a single window. A wet-looking clawed hand is beckoning the players closer through the window.

12 A woman floats atop flotsam from a shipwreck. She cries out for help, saying the captain of her vessel was foolishly taken in by sirens, leaving her stranded. It turns out she's the siren. It's a trap.

13 The players' vessel makes port in a town that is, unbeknownst to the players, the hometown of the most annoying NPC they've ever encountered.

14 Twenty bottles wash up against the ship, all with messages inside. They are all in different languages but all seem to have the same plea for help.

15 A gaggle of sea apes hops on board and entertains with funny dances, cute sounds, and chill vibes. They are a band of thieves and they *will* rob you blind.

16 A mass of strange interconnected ships is quickly gaining on the players' ship. It looks to be seven pirate ships, all moving as one, and these odds seem to be unbeatable. Can they outrun this armada of evil, or will they add their ship to this growing collective?

17 A pirate ship can be seen in the distance, but the typical flag has been replaced with a "Help Wanted" banner. These pirates are low on staff and are very open to the players joining their ranks.

18 In the still of the night, a thick fog rolls in and covers the boat. Strange sounds and lights can be seen moving in the fog. Anyone foolish enough to attempt to find the sounds is attacked by sea pirate ghosts who try to drain their life!

19 The players pass a floating, spiraled shell. Cries for help can be heard inside. If the players break the shell, a figure in a lumpy aqua cloak crawls out. It's the Wodgian Wizard of the Whelk. As thanks, they offer a card with their picture on it. This spell card can surround a target in a nigh-impenetrable whelk shell.

20 A song can be heard on the wind. A chorus of voices is singing to you, filling your mind. This is clearly a siren song, you know that...but damn, it's a bop! The song is really stuck in your head. All the players just want to hear more of the song.

21 The ship slows down and stops with a sickening *schlorp* noise. The sea has taken on an unearthly green tint. Further examination reveals that all the fish just beneath the water are bones.

22 The constellations suddenly become impossibly bright in the sky. The shapes turn into ethereal creatures as the ship rises into the sky. The creatures deliver wisdom to the players (each player gets one question).

23 Huge tidal waves in this section of the ocean mean the players need to do *something* to stabilize the ship. These waves threaten to wreck them.

24 Up ahead are seven boats all tied and moving together. As the players approach, they can hear music, laughter, and general merriment. They've come upon the famous Phelan's Phantastic Party Barge that sails the world.

25 Some surfing aqua goblins challenge the players to "ride one of these gnarly barrels without getting pitted!" They seem to know this area of the ocean well.

26 A giant sea deity gracefully steps across the water. She creates an island in her wake as she passes the players. On the island are countless gorgeous pearls, up for the taking by whoever can swim there the fastest.

27 A strange, mechanical contraption surfaces near the boat. The top opens and a figure with spiral glasses and wild hair emerges. She offers coin to adventurers willing to help find her spouse, who was kidnapped by sharkfolk a day ago. She located the shark hideout, but her beloved doesn't have much more time before their oxygen runs out!

28 A sea god appears to the players, amused at their attempts to cross the ocean. See how a conversation goes between the players and this god.

29 A giant wave forms on the port side of the ship while a large cloud bank forms on the starboard side. An army of giant water elementals has gathered, while giant cloud elementals form in the clouds.

30 Scraping can be heard in the distance. When the players look, they see specters skating over the ocean. Wherever they skate, they leave a trail of ice. If the boat runs into that ice, it could rupture the hull!

31 Some sort of magical spell has made this section of sea a sort of river rapids area. The pace quickens, and steering will be important, as rocks stick out of the water threatening to destroy the ship.

32 A yell can be heard off in the distance from an iceberg, but it sounds muffled. If they get closer, they can see that the iceberg is a humongous ice elemental shouting for everyone to stay away and get out of its path. Oops.

33 Huge blocks of ice are floating in the water. They seem to have been created by an ice elemental off in the distance. If they want to sail through this water, the players will need to deal with the ice elemental first.

34 A shiver of sharks has begun to follow the ship. It turns out that the various crews have been feeding the sharks in this area, so now they follow any ship looking for an easy meal. If they don't get anything, the sharks will start slamming the ship.

35 A strange metal fish surfaces next to the ship and fires a harpoon into the boat. A hatch opens up, and pirates begin attacking the ship and trying to steal the cargo.

36 A cold front moves in with uncanny speed. Suddenly, an iceberg can be seen in the distance. Weirdly, the iceberg seems to be moving toward the players. The players soon realize this iceberg is actually the fin of a glacier shark on the hunt!

37 The ship comes upon a naval blockade. The captain of the main ship demands the party submit to being questioned, boarded, and searched.

38 The group suddenly shudders with a chill as they hear a sickening screech from the bottom of the boat. As they look out, they see the entire ocean has been frozen solid.

39 Cries for help can be heard in the distance. Looking to the horizon, a figure can barely be seen with fins circling around them. If the players don't get over there soon, this might be that poor person's last swim.

40 A noise off the port side is actually a new steam-powered boat piloted by a gnome and her crew. She is willing to sell you an engine, but the ship will have to stop for a few days while it's installed. She promises five times the speed once they are done.

41 Fish begin jumping at the boat. At first, it seems like a boon, as food will now be less scarce, but then someone gets bitten. Jumping piranhas are attacking the players! How do the players defend themselves from the ravenous horde?

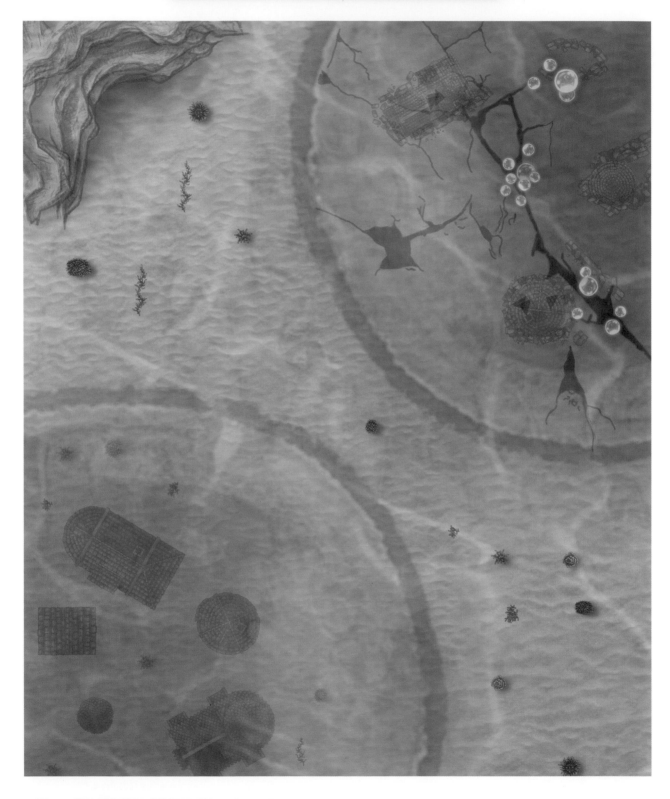

42 A giant coral reef juts out of the ocean nearby. A wide variety of magical and intelligent sea life lives in and around this reef. The ship needs to steer clear if the players wish to avoid wrecking the reef.

43 A big merperson pops out of the water, excited to see an adventuring group in the area. They need help. A vampire octopus has begun attacking their village. They offer potions to enable underwater breathing and a sizeable payment for the players' help.

44 A floating breakfast stand sells seanut butter and jellyfish sandwiches along with lots of other early-morning delicacies of the sea. Each one will impart the diner with some sea-based ability for a limited time.

45 The players can see a vast city shimmering under the waves. Odd as it is, there is a domed city of land-dwelling species living here just under the surface.

46 A gaggle of mermen approach the ship and are eager to talk about the world of dry land. They are also eager to share all of the gossip they know about the creatures in the sea and the ships they have seen recently.

47 Bubbles on the surface indicate something big underneath the waves. Underwater is a giant glass dome with cracks letting air out. Entering, the players see the remnants of a prosperous city. Signs indicate there was recently some kind of catastrophe. There are giant, bulky suits of armor wandering around that seem to be a form of security for the city. These sentries set upon any living thing walking in the open.

48 An underwater lava vent makes this the perfect habitat for merdwarves (half-dwarf, half-octopus creatures). They offer some strong sea hooch to the weary travelers and invite the group to their underwater cave "if ye can find a way to breathe there...ye ken?"

49 The water near this coral reef is magically breathable! The players have the opportunity to stop at an undersea tavern, swim with sea creatures, and stock up on supplies.

50 A friendly sea otter bobs up to the ship clapping and making a commotion. It seems like it wants the group to follow it. If they do, they find a mermaid child trapped at the bottom of an air-pocket under the sea. The child will suffocate if not returned to the water soon!

51 As the party explores a small cove, they notice a large group of diverse sea creatures in the middle of some sort of celebration. They are celebrating the wedding of their princess, who has married a land prince. The sea creatures will invite the party to join in the fun, for on this day only, the sea gods have granted all animals the ability to breathe both on land and in water.

52 A group of strange fishfolk approaches the ship in large bubbles. They offer to take the players to their underwater city to trade and share knowledge.

53 A sea-merchant dinghy pulls up to the adventurers. They sell many provisions and wares, including potions for water breathing, flippers, and a regal-looking trident that they refuse to give any details about.

54 It's a relatively quiet night when suddenly something big hits the underside of the boat and the ship starts taking on water!

55 The ship rocks as tentacles rise from the water. A kraken is attacking! Fortunately, it's a small one...maybe even a baby? Which may mean that the mother is nearby.

56 A child is struggling in the water. After being rescued, they cry that their sibling was swallowed by a huge monster! They ask you to "go into the monster's tummy" to rescue their loved one.

57 A herd of water horses is galloping across the surface of the water just east of the ship. They can be caught and travel on water faster than any ship, but they can't leave the water or they will cease to exist.

58 In the distance, the players can see a whale surface. Of note, when the whale clears its blowhole, golden coins come shooting out.

59 Everyone has been noticing an extreme increase in static shock today. Looking over the bow confirms why: The water is slithering with thousands of electric eels. Don't touch the water!

60 The boat suddenly drops as a giant mouth engulfs the ship. The players have been eaten whole by some kind of sea monster. How will they escape?

61 This island looks like a giant octopus sticking out of the water, its long tentacles spread out into the sea. There's a cave where an eye might be, and inside is a glowing emerald gem the size of a human head. If anyone removes the gem from the cave, the whole island comes to life as a giant octopus and tries to sink the ship.

62 A giant, floating corpse bumps against the ship's hull. The stench is nearly unbearable, but a magic-looking pink goo is pouring from the mouth. If the party dares to venture inside, they find it crawling with living pink goo monsters, and also find this creature had an appetite for ships, which have somehow remained mostly intact.

63 The players find a stowaway on the ship. It seems a very curious creature hid away on the ship at their last landing. The creature has an insatiable appetite and equally unquenchable curiosity. Much chaos ensues as the adorable but pesky animal rearranges items all across the ship.

64 A bird person lands on the deck of the ship. They introduce themself as Nephele, a wizard who is making their way to help out another kingdom. They offer to tell stories of their travels in exchange for resting here for the day before moving on.

65 An incredible voice can be heard singing in the distance. The lyrics reference sadness and sickness (both of the heart and the body). A muse on a nearby shore has been separated from her girlfriend. Being apart is making her physically ill.

66 A day into the trip, the entire crew abandons the players on the ship in the middle of the night. The crew has taken everything they can carry. There are the barest of supplies left and definitely not enough to last the whole trip.

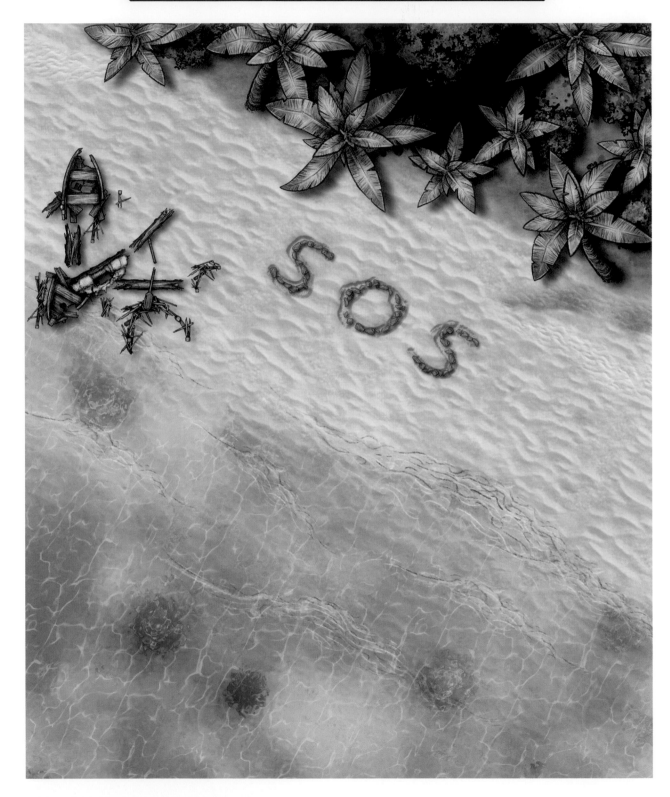

67 One night just after midnight, the players are awakened by chanting. On the ship's deck, the captain has drawn arcane runes and circles all over the deck and is chanting in a strange language. He's offering up the crew and the players to a dark ocean god to gain eternal life and power.

68 Harpoons can be spotted poised on the edges of a nearby island. They seem to be shooting into the ocean. Long, low-pitched screams can be heard rumbling from below the surface. It seems this island's inhabitants are hunting whale-folk.

69 As a flock of seagulls flies overhead, one dives into the ship. When it hits the mast, it explodes! Suddenly, all of the seagulls turn to attack the ship in the same way. Some villain has learned how to weaponize the seagulls against the players!

70 A large makeshift sign on a nearby island reads "SOS." If the players travel to the island, most of the inhabitants are zombies. A few survivors are in a tall treehouse toward the center of the island.

71 A beautiful coastline can be seen in the distance. This place is a popular vacation destination catering only to the wealthiest patrons. Unfortunately, the ambiance is currently being wrecked by legions of monstrous leeches covering the beaches.

72 There is a legend of a magical island that can only be reached when the stars are in proper alignment. A local wizard has engaged the services of the players to help them reach the island and defeat the many magical creatures along the way that protect the island from outside intruders. It's dangerous work, but the reward for making it to the island could be immense.

73 The sea current turns hostile, washing the ship up on a deserted island. All the animals here have a strange purple aura, and attack with vicious anger. Toward the center of the island, foliage is wilted and the ground glows a sickly purple.

74 The ship captain knows that there should be a lighthouse near where they are but can't see the light. The captain fears something is terribly wrong and asks the players to investigate.

75 The players hear about a boy who went missing on a nearby island, and the big reward for his safe return. No one who has gone to find the boy ever returns. In reality, the boy is a powerful sorcerer who ran away from home, casting charm spells on anyone who comes to bring him back. The charmed adventurers live a comfortable island life protecting their new boy king.

76 An island in the distance is getting closer faster than seems possible with the speed of the ship. It is an island on the back of a large turtle, and the villagers who live there are eager to talk and trade.

77 A terrible storm destroys the ship. The players wash up on an uninviting, dangerous island, all separated from each other.

78 A heavy storm at sea forces the ship to find shelter within a large grotto. Inside the grotto is a small fishing village in which all revere Mother Seaspray, their healer and rumored witch. Mother is willing to allow the crew to anchor in the grotto but will only let a few people come to shore and look around the village. Snooping around reveals bounty posters for Mother Seaspray worth 30,000 gold for her capture dead or alive.

79 A woman in flowing blue robes stands atop a 50-foot-tall water spout skimming across the water, heading straight for the ship. A mass of sharks is swimming around in the twirling water spout. She hovers her spout next to the ship and introduces herself as Arabelle the Water Witch and says she is curious about the players' travels. If the players' quest sounds noble, she will let them have a magical compass. If she deems them treacherous, she will let loose her sharks to attack.

80 Plumes of boiling water start bubbling up and rocking the boat, spraying the decks with scalding hot water. Soon, lava imps start attaching themselves to the boat, attempting to pull themselves out of the water to avoid becoming rock. Unfortunately, they are burning through the ship.

81 The ship comes upon an outcropping of rock that has four dire rainbow shrimp that are protecting their territory. They start firing off their supersonic punches and quickly start breaking parts of the ship into pieces.

82 As night falls, light begins to shine from *under* the boat. As the group looks out, they can see bioluminescent algae shining everywhere on top of the ocean. The glow seems to form a trail off the path the group has been sailing on.

83 A fish circus swims up to the ship and starts performing amazing acts of swimming and some aerial acrobatics. They toss up a scroll asking for donations for their treasure trove.

84 A school of dolphins swims next to the ship. They are hyperintelligent and are amused at the players' attempts at primitive communication with them.

85 A gigantic fish with a human face flops against the boat and tells the group that if they answer a riddle, the fish will grant the party one wish. The stipulation here is that the fish is not magically powerful, so it has pretty serious limitations as far as wish fulfillment.

86 A large dragon crash-lands on the deck of the ship, clearly wounded and angry. It lashes out at anyone who gets too close but quickly passes out from its wounds.

87 A strange figure is approaching the ship, slowly, as if they are walking. He's a kindly old man named Izie on a pilgrimage to an island temple. He was told by his god that he must walk there.

88 The crew and the players are deeply confused as they see a ship just like the one they are on heading straight for them. The captain tries to turn, but the other ship matches the captain's movements perfectly. As the other ship draws close, everyone can see themselves. Somehow the way forward is blocked by a giant mirrored force field.

89 On the horizon, a large castle made out of coral can be seen floating on the water. The population of this castle is very diverse, having gathered people from their travels around the world and deep in the sea. The merchants here have items from everywhere in the world for sale.

90 After a successful day, the ship's crew invites the players to eat, drink, and be merry as they throw a simple but very drunken party. Toward the end of the evening, one of the crew members leans over the edge of the ship and falls into the ocean. Can the players save them in their drunken state?

91 A naval ship is stopped dead in the sea. The captain of the naval ship, Tatiana Bach, is overjoyed to be saved but says that her whole crew was killed by the dread pirate Robin "The Vulture" Ashes. She demands to commandeer the ship to chase down Ashes for her kingdom. She promises a very handsome reward.

92 Several weather-beaten boats are tangled together, floating adrift. A few survivors aboard have a terrible tale of a whirlpool nearly killing them all. They are desperate to be saved but panic when the winds pick up and the waters become very choppy. A large school of fish is frantically swimming nearby, but are they the cause of the calamity or a symptom?

93 Suddenly, a gigantic mound of cooling lava bursts through the surface of the water, forming a new island. The party watches as a large leaf unfurls in the middle of the new land. From this leaf springs forth a sprite that starts planting the seeds that will make this island a desirable destination for travelers. The sprite seems happy to have company and will gladly take advice on how best to terraform the island.

94 The party awakens one morning to find that the ship is no longer rocking gently in the ocean waves. It is sitting at the muddy bottom of the ocean. The water is forming a seemingly endless wall all around the ship. The sun is barely visible, as if at the end of the long water tunnel. The silhouette of strange creatures can be seen staring out at the ship from inside the walls of water.

95 The captain has a drum he says will beat whenever something dangerous is nearby, but the crew says no one has ever heard the drum. Most don't believe it's really magic. Then one night, the drum starts beating.

96 While fishing off the side of the ship, a crew member drags up something large from deep in the sea. It's a large barrel that explodes when it touches the air. The captain screams that they must have floated into a pirate minefield and that they need to pull up all fishing lines and turn the boat immediately.

97 A thick fog rolls in, obscuring the route. When the fog lifts, the sky is black, compromising the ship's navigation. What do the players do to make sure they are still on course?

98 A fiery object plummets from the sky and lands just off the port bow with a giant splash that rocks the boat. Those that investigate find a strange egg with an elven baby inside. A note asks whoever finds the child to keep them safe until they are strong enough to return home.

99 The players pass by a huge vessel. They hear upbeat music booming from inside the hull. The ship seems to be full of people partying. If investigated, it seems the patrons here can do nothing except dance and party. They are unable to communicate with the players except to grimace in rare moments of understanding.

100 A beautiful island of pink sand and blue foliage can be spied in the distance. The residents are all extremely generous, offering the players anything they want, sometimes without reason or request. They seem genuinely innocent.

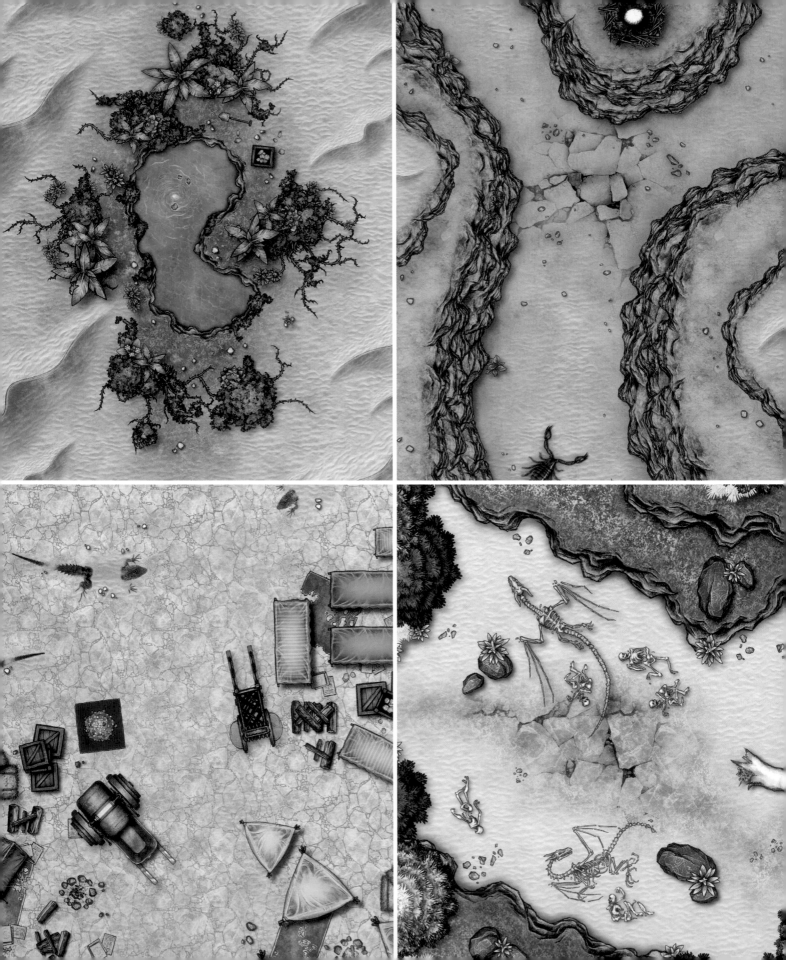

DESERT

In a barren desert, it behooves you as the GM to have a handle on what the area lacks and what it has in abundance. This area is defined by what's not there; namely, water, food, or shelter.

That's a great place to start when you're trying to feel out what the stakes are in a desert encounter. A quick fight with a beast is hardly a problem in the woods, but put that beast in the desert, and characters will leave the fight parched and starved.

Scarcity isn't the only thing the desert has going for it though. Deserts have a ton of open space, more so than just about anywhere else. That makes them ideal settings for anything that requires a lot of room. Gladiatorial combat, scenes with massive creatures, and vehicle-based encounters thrive here for that reason.

Focusing your scene narration on things beyond just what objects and landmarks the players see in the desert can help make otherwise drab desert scenes pop. What faraway giant animal sounds might pierce through the air, unimpeded by forests or structures? And an encounter under the blistering midday heat is suddenly much different if you change it to take place in the dark during the desert's freezing night temperatures.

The oasis is a moment of rest, the mirage is your chance to explore the characters' desires, and a looming sandstorm can add urgency to any encounter.

1 A crowd has formed around a crater in the sands. Apparently, a fireball from the sky hit this area a while back, melting the sand into glass. Now it's an ultra-smooth crater where the most radical desert denizens compete in the new sport, roll-planking. The leader is a huge djinn who challenges the players to show her a sick stunt. If they do, she'll grant them a wish.

2 A tribe of lion people uses this rock outcropping in the middle of the desert as their home base. They are friendly but not very generous, as their supplies are meager.

3 A blue bottle sticks out of the sand. It's cold to the touch, and there is liquid inside. If uncorked, an ocean's worth of freezing cold water begins pouring out at unreal speed. It won't stop until it is recorked.

4 A small field of dark purple roses grows out of the sand. If touched, the sand around each rose drops as a sand angler's jaws snap around the flower.

5 A relaxed community of sentient, crawling cactus people race each other across obstacle courses on giant dune bugs. They challenge the players to a race.

6 The players encounter an outlaw with a bag of gold, no more water, and only an hour's head start on the mercenaries the bank hired to get their funds back. The outlaw will split the pot fifty-fifty with the players if they take care of the mercenaries for him.

7 Massive tumbleweeds terrorize these sands. They are not magical. They are not alive. They merely blow with the wind. They also clump together to form massive spiky murder waves that puncture at speed and impede travel at rest.

8 The sand turns pink then gradually a deep red. Eventually, the players come to the source: some sort of maw in the floor of the desert that is spewing out blood.

9 A sandstorm is coming. The players will need to set up a shelter to protect themselves until it passes over.

10 An out-of-place paved road leads out of eyesight. If the players travel down the road, they see a huge stone palace. Gila behemoths are crawling all over the building, but the players can also see gold glimmering everywhere.

11 A giant statue towers over the sands. Half dwarf, half bear. This must be one of the dwear from history books.

12 This desert lake is the only source of water for miles. The players see three villages spread out around the lake. All three are under a strange curse. Village one is only awake from midnight to 8 a.m., village two is awake from 8 a.m. to 4 p.m., and the last village is awake from 4 p.m. to midnight. The curse can be broken if all three villages work together to build one monument over one full day.

13 A towering sprawl of ancient ribs sticks out of the sand here. As the group passes, the ground shakes and sand pits form as the gargantuan skeleton reanimates. It seems angry.

14 In the distance, a resplendent ship can be seen. Seems like this area used to be an ocean. There might still be something of worth inside!

15 The big wave up ahead is *not* a mirage. The players have reached the coast, and that's a tsunami!

16 Any moving parts of armor, weapons, means of transport, and crevices of *any* kind are completely full of sand. It's affecting most aspects of life negatively and the group needs to figure out a way to deal with the grit that has gathered everywhere.

17 A sign reading "Now Entering the Dry Dunes" does not provide enough warning of the withered zombies that roam the land.

18 Up ahead, the players can see something glinting in the sunlight. It seems to be lifelike human statues made out of glass. Slithering under the sands is a creature that will turn anything to glass with just one look.

19 One of the players falls into magical quicksand. Unfortunately, this stuff acts like quicksand does in cartoons. It's a massive vortex pulling the player down.

20 This small desert town is a relief to find. The fact that the buildings are oddly very cool is an added benefit. However, this marvel of cooling is a result of small boxes that house winter spirits.

21 A whirlwind of sand speeds toward the players. The wind dies as it gets close, and Rue the Sand Witch, dressed in swirling red scarves, stops to ask the players why they are trespassing in her desert. If treated well, she will take them to her hovel and let them recuperate for the night. If they upset her, she will attempt to bury them in the sands.

22 A giant stone tomb stands as a monolith in the sands. Anyone approaching hears screams in their head, spirits begging to be released. If the players enter the tomb, they are locked in a dungeon along with the screaming spirits.

23 A small outcropping of homes is the home of a family of elves who forage the desert for precious metals and stones, farm an odd assortment of cacti that grow strange fruit, and rent out sand sails for crossing the dunes.

24 The players come upon a group of trolls playing volleyball. They are having an impromptu tournament.

25 Just after sundown, a small dark cloud is quickly moving toward the players. A cloud of vampiric bats is out and looking for blood.

26 The party finds the wreckage of a crashed airship. The expensive cargo is still intact but all food and survival gear are gone. The last entry in the ship's log notes the crew is going north to find help.

27 Off in the distance, the players see pyramids. The largest pyramid has a great eye hovering above it that can communicate telepathically. It tells the players to enter the pyramid and set the creature there free for a handsome reward. The creature considers consuming the party a great reward.

28 A rock that looks like a shark fin sticks out of the ground. Inspection of the rock reveals that it is attached to a dead sand shark, but the fins are moving.

29 Up ahead is a rare sight: a river in the middle of the desert. There is a large group of humanoid elephants gathering water and bathing in the river. The guards of this group are very alert and will defend their families to the death. The players must be extremely careful to not start a fight with these fierce warriors.

30 As the players fill up water skins at an oasis, the terrain turns sinister. This is some kind of illusion, but it isn't a mirage; the poisonous creatures crawling toward the adventurers are real.

31 The players keep seeing a figure in a lumpy pink cloak shimmering into and out of view. The figure attempts to introduce themself, but it's too garbled to hear. The figure must have gotten lost in the mirage realm. If the players free the figure, they introduce themself as the Wodgian Wizard of the Wisp. As thanks, they offer a card with their picture on it. This spell card can open a portal to the mirage realm.

32 A band of goblins riding ostriches attacks the players. They circle the party on their fast-moving mounts, darting in and out, trying to stab the players or capture them in nets. If they start to lose the battle, they will quickly flee.

33 The players find a body of water as blue as the sky. Everything in it floats, and the water tastes very salty. Anyone who drinks it will be poisoned, but braver players can try bobbing on the surface of the water. Just don't stay in too long!

34 The players find themselves in the path of a stampede of camels. If the players can deal with the monsters chasing the camels, they'd have the perfect ride.

35 An oasis is within sight. There, the players discover the plants and animals are prickly and aggressively defend their territory. If these threats can be cleared out, it could be a wonderful place to rest.

36 Buzzard bears are circling overhead. Unlike regular buzzards, they won't just wait for their prey to die.

37 The players are out of water. They need to find a source of fresh water soon. Their thirst is starting to impact every aspect of life.

38 There is a water tournament happening at this lake in the middle of the desert. The winners gain control of the next year's fishing rights. A village elder approaches the players. They think one of the other villages is planning to cheat. They want the party to investigate.

39 An oasis is visible in the distance. The players could use rest and a water refill... but first, they'll have to get through the spiny coyotes that occupy this small, lush area.

40 A rumble in the distance gets the players' attention. They see a sand wake behind a moving sand dune. Undoubtedly, a sand wyrm is headed their way.

41 An oasis spirit at the players' camp requests protection from the mining company threatening to destroy the oasis in search of diamonds underneath.

42 A sudden, torrential downpour soaks the sand, making movement much harder. A wizard nearby is attempting experiments to transform this area into a lush jungle.

43 The players can see a small pool of water up ahead and some weird heat waves coming from that area. Upon arrival, they see a pack of fire imps that is attacking a pack of water imps. If the players don't help, the water imps will be destroyed and the water will evaporate away. The water imps are grateful and reward anyone who helps.

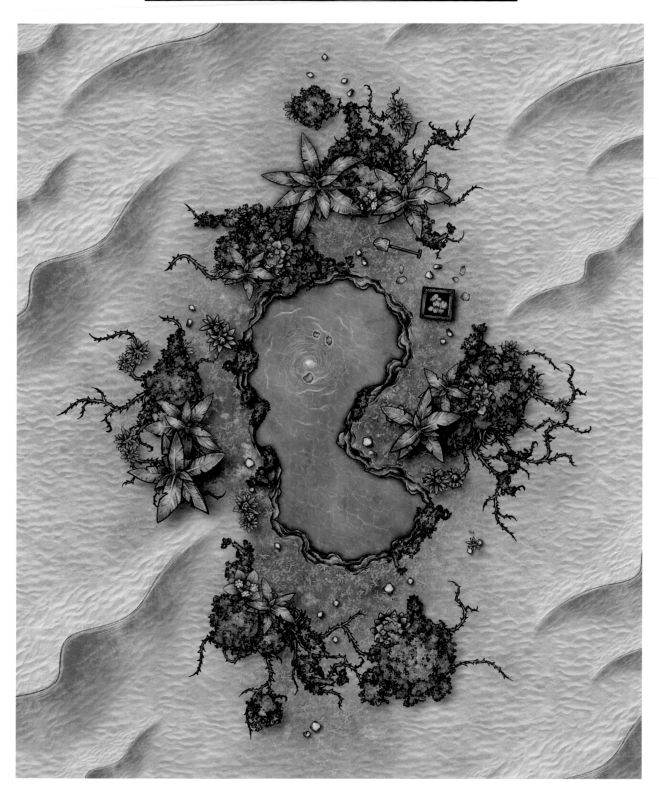

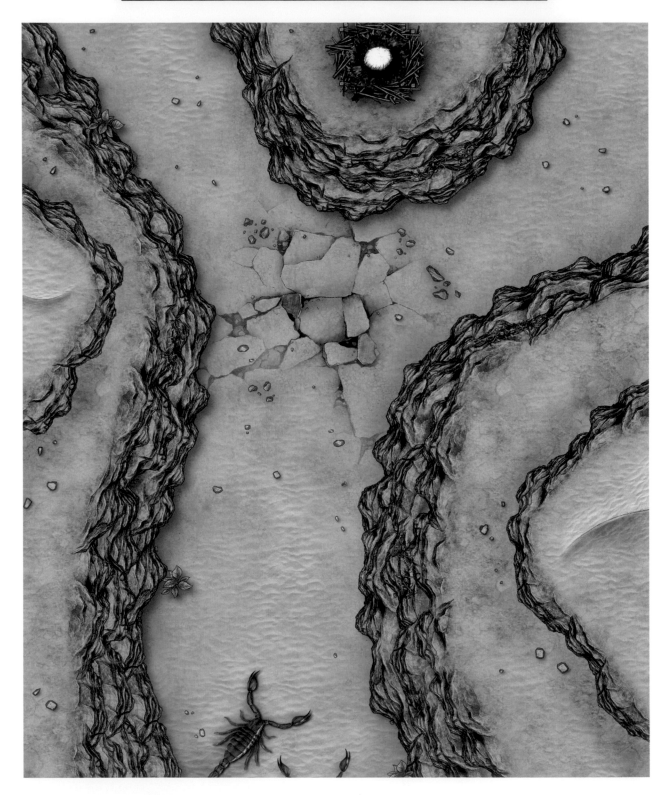

44 While walking through a long canyon, the players are harassed by a tribe of goblins trying to get their hands on anything and everything they can.

45 A massive rock outcropping is the pedestal for a giant nest. Inside the nest is one egg that is shaking a bit. A sudden shadow alerts the players to the roc that is returning home.

46 This rocky ravine gives the perfect shade to make this section of desert travel faster and much easier. Halfway through the ravine, the skies darken suddenly and torrents of rain begin to fall. The ravine is suddenly inundated with water and becomes a raging river within minutes.

47 A group of terrified people stands atop a large rock outcropping frantically waving at you and urging your party to run. A quick glance behind you shows something moving through the sand toward you extremely fast.

48 Tonight is the one night of the year when this incredibly rare cactus's flowers bloom. A huge crowd of plant enthusiasts has gathered. Legends say watching the cactus bloom drives its watcher wild with terrifying hallucinations along with untold pleasures.

49 A dog has been following the group. It's emaciated and dehydrated. It is curious of anyone offering food and water, but is hesitant at first. The dog will love the group forever if they show it kindness.

50 The players realize with some dread that a group of giant scorpions is stalking them. The creatures seem to be skilled hunters and are cutting off potential escape routes.

51 An outcropping of rocks makes for an easier path than the sand the party has been trudging through, until the footing becomes shaky. One of the rocks stands up to become a Rock Titan. The individual pieces of the creature float by magic. The creature seems to be guarding something.

52 Everyone has been in this desert too long. Sunburns are turning to sun poisoning. Maybe it's a delusion, but the players could swear there's a small army of weapons approaching. They are spinning and flourishing all on their own without wielders.

53 A bored giant sphinx lights up when the players approach. The sphinx mentions how tired they are of riddles; they want, instead, to hold a poetry competition. Each player can write a short poem to impress the sphinx.

54 Rocks jut up out of the sand dune like large wicked-looking claws reaching for the sun. As the players walk near, the rocks bend and twist like tentacles as a giant sand squid emerges from the shifting sands. Its rock-like appendages attempt to grab the players.

55 A village built around an oasis can be seen in the distance. The locals are a strange species none of the players have seen before. They have odd customs but are welcoming.

56 The players stumble upon an enormous dragon asleep on a large rock in the bright sun. With the sand muffling their footsteps, it would be easy to get away without waking the dragon. But on the other hand, how often do you get the chance to surprise a sleeping dragon?

57 The party is making its way through salt flats. The player walking at the front of the group steps on a camouflaged giant horned salt lizard, and it is extremely displeased. Emitting a hissing shriek, the creature awakens its nearby lizard friends, and they all attack the group.

58 As the players approach a ghost town next to a mostly dried-up oasis, it looks like the whole area is covered in spiderwebs. However, the strands are the shed skin of the large rattlesnakes that inhabit this abandoned town.

59 While walking across the salt flats, the players hear strange mechanical sounds ahead. They come across a gnomish mechanical carriage drag race. The winner gets 100 gold.

60 The cactus water everyone drank appears to have some *additional* properties. Everyone sees the world melting before their eyes. That's when a giant sand-shifter attacks.

61 There is a festival happening in the center of these salt flats. Pilgrims are using their wagons and extra supplies to build giant effigies of their gods. They plan to burn them on the final day of the festival. They will then walk the desert back home as part of their pilgrimage. They are encouraging you to do the same to find enlightenment.

62 A pack of spirits from an extinct desert species stalks the players. When they roar, the spirits manifest more strongly, revealing brief glimpses of what their appearance was when they lived.

63 There are three villages around this large oasis. Each village specializes in items and enchantments around one of the four elements. There is a village of fishfolk at the bottom of the lake who cover all things water.

64 A gnomish inventor hires the players to come out to the salt flats and hold up long metal poles in a thunderstorm to test a theory.

65 There are three villages around this large lake oasis. Only one is ever occupied at a time. The residents swap villages every five years and today is Moving Day! A wealthy family wants the players to help them get the best house in the new village. No killing allowed, but everything else is open.

66 Spread out around the edge of the salt flats are many camps, each with its own colored tents and flag. In each encampment is a diverse group of peoples. Asking any of them reveals this is an annual swap meet festival for the next five days. On the fifth day, there is a giant battle in the center of the encampments to decide which clan rules for that year.

67 A tear in reality opens up, and someone in strange clothes walks out. They say they are from the future, sent here to avoid a catastrophe directly related to the players.

68 A meteor sizzles in the sky above before the players hear and feel a huge explosion. If they travel to the meteor's crash site, they find a crater in the dunes with a very strange individual at the center.

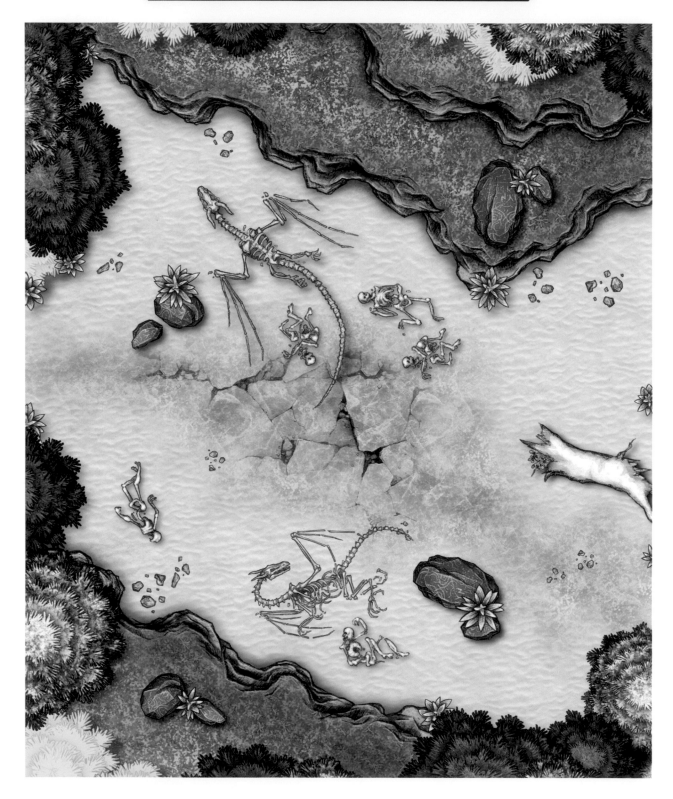

69 This night has gone on for too long. The cold of night in the desert is becoming more and more extreme. Frost forms in the players' nostrils. What has happened to the sun?

70 A collection of dried-out bones lies sun-bleached in the sand. As the players draw near, the bones animate into a giant lizard-like skeleton that roars in an otherworldly tongue.

71 During the cold night, the party is traveling over frozen tundra. Something strange is stuck in the ground here. If the players dig up or otherwise disturb the object, it stirs to life, pulsating and hovering a few feet off the ground. It is a mass of strange and shifting matter, the color of which is something altogether unfamiliar to the players. The entity communicates directly with the characters' minds through feelings. Everyone shudders as they realize this thing is out to destroy *everything*.

72 The ground gives way to a whirlpool of shifting sand as an enormous antlion eagerly awaits the vortex to drag everyone down to be eaten.

73 A sudden, out of place flurry of snow bursts from a tear in the very air. Gusts of freezing cold flow from this tear, freezing the ground and letting out strange extra-dimensional beasts of fractal ice. These ice beings feed by draining warmth from anything nearby.

74 Giant pillars dot the horizon ahead and the heat seems particularly intense around them. If anyone gets within 500 feet of the pillars, giant fire ants pour out.

75 A large forest of what looks to be dead trees lies ahead. The trees themselves are actually made of stone, and the dryads who tend to them are willing to trade precious gems.

76 As the sun sets, the temperature plummets and the terrain shifts to a dry tundra. Skeletons of various creatures large and small litter the landscape. Just as the sunset completes, all the skeletons animate and attack anything nearby.

77 A large vehicle that looks like a giant brick on tank wheels trundles toward the players. The hauler stops near the players, and a small group comes out to sell the party the items they have found throughout the desert. For the right price, they will let the party into the hauler for a short trek across the dunes.

78 The players come upon a large skeleton that is clearly the bones of a long-dead dragon. Its hoard is nearby, guarded by its three adolescent children.

79 This verdant mesa is a welcome find. A small winding path leads up to a wondrous jungle atop the mesa. A tribe of druids lives here and keeps this place as a sanctuary for travelers and animals lost in the desert. They are adamant that no hunting happen within the mesa.

80 A city stands inside a large glass globe. The elves and humans inside seem to be comfortable and are walking down lanes filled with greenery and lush fruit trees. If the players want to enter, they must turn over all their weapons and magic items for the duration of their stay.

81 A small temple sits at the bank of a desert river; its heat-baked clay exterior visually melds into the sand dunes around it. The building is simple in design without any extra decoration or adornments outside. Inside is a pool of refreshing water brought up from the river and five humanoid turtle monks, most of whom are in deep meditation next to the basin of water. They are peaceful.

82 The river is a welcome relief from the hot sand and blazing sun. The water is cool and deep. The players can see animals up and down the river banks, drinking the water but keeping their distance. If anyone drinks or enters the water, a school of tiger fish with vicious teeth attacks anyone in the water.

83 At the base of this mesa is a series of buildings and homes carved out of stone set into the walls of the mesa itself. Black smoke pours out of a few of the doorways, and screams can be heard from the citizens of this town. A band of marauders on camelback have attacked this town and are stealing and killing with abandon.

84 The sand here has drained into the ground and now resembles a giant bleached skull gazing into the heavens. Where the mouth would be on the skull is a cave entrance that leads down into darkness. A whisper on the wind warns them that only the pure of heart can leave the caves of sorrow alive.

85 A corked flask sticks up out of the sand. It is making a strange buzzing sound, but the outside is opaque so the contents can't be seen. Anyone uncorking the flask unleashes a torrent of flesh-eating beetles that swarms and attacks the players. Only recorking the flask will stop the endless stream of biting bugs.

86 A river flows through this area of the desert, creating a line of foliage that's a little out of place. As the players near the river, silt elementals plod up from the verdant ground, covered in foliage, ready to defend this area from intruders.

87 The players come across a clockwork knight standing frozen and half buried in the sand. Its gears are caked in sand and dust. The knight holds a scroll clamped tightly in its closed metal hand. If repaired, the knight immediately returns to walking across the desert to deliver a letter of love it was commanded to take to a long-dead prince.

88 The players come across a ship graveyard. Thirty sailing ships are stuck in the sand, broken and burnt. The ships look hundreds of years old but still have a few sealed casks inside their cargo holds. Is it possible that this whole area was once part of a vast ocean?

89 Up ahead is a large river with a ferry boat floating by. A group of humanoid hippos is on the boat, fending off dire crocodiles taking out chunks of the boat. Should the players help the hippos, they are more than happy to escort them up or down river. They can also offer maps of the area for easier travel.

90 Just as the players arrive at this oasis town, they see a large stage with an auctioneer and a strong, handsome, shirtless guy being auctioned off. It's this town's annual bachelor and bachelorette auction. There are a wide variety of other tribes, races, and traveling parties that are here to take part in the fun. The town views it as a cultural exchange and divides the profits among the leaders who help sponsor the event.

91 A pride of lionfolk is chasing after the players; their roars are fierce and terrifying. Once they catch up, they demand that the players turn out their bags. They are looking for the Jewel of a Thousand Sunrises, the very object the players were hired to find from a very deadly dungeon.

92 Brilliant streaks of red and blue sand suddenly appear and swirl around the players' feet. The sand dances around them before both streaks dart off in opposite directions. These are the impish sands that like to play with travelers of the dunes. It is said that the blue sands lead to water but the red sands lead to gold beyond imagining.

93 A figure on a windsurfing board glides by on the dunes. They have several hand-painted sand gliders for sale. Honestly, they are probably undercharging for this detail work. Damn, these boards are incredible! You should let them know they should charge more. Quality art is worth paying for!

94 An ornate sarcophagus is sticking haphazardly out of the ground. Pulling it out of the sand takes effort. There is no body inside, just numerous gold items and artifacts. If the players take any items, a mummy begins to hunt the party to retrieve the items it had while alive.

95 A flash of light in the sky catches the players' eyes. A small mechanical owl is flying past and desperately trying to outrun the half-man, half-scorpion creature that is chasing it. The owl will try to land with the party for protection and the scorpion man will demand the owl. If the party saves the owl, the owl tells them of its gnomish maker and where to find her house of wonders within this vast desert.

96 A large snake creature bursts out of a sand dune far ahead of the players, its red and purple body surrounded by electrical discharge as it dives back into the sand. Small bolts of lightning mark where it dove back in before it re-emerges even closer to the party, filling the area with electricity. It doesn't attack, but its random movements and the electrical field it leaves behind are incredibly dangerous.

97 A group of gnomes is tossing a bunch of lava imps up in the air so that they slam into the sand. They then collect the glass that is left behind after the impact. The gnomes swear that they aren't hurting the imps, who do seem to enjoy the process. The gnomes will make the party any glass items they want if they help with their collection process.

98 The players come upon a set of dehydrated corpses of a previous adventuring party that had made this same journey. A few belongings are left in their bags buried in the sand, one of which is a diary. The diary outlines almost the same set of circumstances that led the players here.

99 An enormous clod of dirt is quickly rolling toward the party. It is easy to avoid, as the dire dung beetle that is pushing it has no interest in the party, only in its prize. There are rumors that the shells of dung beetles make light and easy armor, but also, where did it get a poo that size?

100 A large *boom* is heard in the distance. The players find a bunch of dwarves who are testing their new barrel bombs. If the players help out, they offer gold or one bomb as a reward. However, testing seems to be a dangerous prospect.

PART TWO

GAME MASTER TOOLS

Encounter scenarios are great at giving your RPG session structure and tone, but they're far from all you need for a great game. With that in mind, these sections of game master tools fill your session with those extra details, like colorful non-player characters, exciting settings, or unpredictable magical effects.

NPC GENERATION

Non-player characters (NPCs) are one of the greatest tools available to a GM. You can use them to nudge the players in a certain narrative direction, to teach them about the story and world, or to just be a friend to the party. This table has one hundred NPC concepts— everything from physical descriptions to backstories—that you can use when preparing a session, or on the fly by rolling one up mid-session.

LOCATION

No adventure occurs in a vacuum! If you're not sure where to set an encounter, or it's the middle of a session and you feel like the narrative needs a change of scenery, this table of one hundred locations has you covered.

D100	LOCATION
1	This place clearly used to be the site of many fancy parties, but the joy of the past has given way to dust, cobwebs, and ruin.
2	A magic show is being performed for children nearby. They all think the encounter is part of the act.
3	This is a city hall for the local form of government.
4	A tavern where all the patrons have had way too many and are spoiling for a fight.

D100	LOCATION
5	A clothing shop with lots of places to hide.
6	A brilliant palace with guards who don't abide trespassers.
7	An arena with jeering crowds that can affect the battle with their enthusiasm or disdain.
8	A damaged sailing ship washed up on shore.
9	A crater where something from another world landed long ago.
10	A forest that is currently ablaze. Desperate animals trying to escape create hazards at regular intervals.
11	An extravagant party. The players have reason not to disturb the guests.

D100	LOCATION	D100	LOCATION
12	A long-forgotten, crude surgery room with lots of rusted, scary-looking instruments.	27	A dark cavern with beautiful gemstones embedded into the walls.
13	The back of an enormous beast. If characters fall, they may get hurt and will need to work to catch up.	28	A noble family's mausoleum in the center of a beautifully tended cemetery.
14	A delicately balanced platform on a small pedestal. If the weight shifts significantly to one side, everyone could fall.	29	The edge of a ravine that drops 200 feet down.
15	A body of water with large lily pads that can support the weight of a few people.	30	A large circular room, 50 feet in diameter. Shelving lines the walls, filled with an odd assortment of books and baubles.
16	A barn filled with volatile explosives.	31	A riotous beer garden outside of a middle-of-the-road tavern. Long picnic tables dominate the space.
17	A dimly lit mansion with a deep, dark basement.	32	An unfortunate clearing of dead trees and grass in an otherwise vibrant and lively forest.
18	A misty forest, densely packed with trees and easy to get lost in.	33	A circle of wagons and carriages off the side of the road getting ready to tuck in for the night.
19	A snowy mountain peak with a fantastic view just as the sun is setting.	34	A large warehouse on the pier packed full of ill-gotten goods, with narrow walkways and paths through the space.
20	A local fair with lots of large mechanical rides, game booths, and sideshows.	35	A rocky outcropping on the coastline that looks like the hollowed skull of a giant.
21	A busy tavern with a live band playing loudly.	36	A silver-and-glass-globed city under the sea.
22	The edge of a cliff with a lengthy fall for anyone who loses their footing.	37	The smelly, rat-infested sewers of a run-down section of the city.
23	A tall tower with a spiral staircase to the top.	38	The inner courtyard and battle arena for the local magic school.
24	Housing and other buildings in treetops, navigated via the many vines that hang down.	39	Winter, deep in the forest; a gentle snowfall makes everything quiet and eerie.
25	A large, moving wagon with spooked horses at the front pulling at full speed.	40	A weather-beaten cottage on a lonely island with one dead tree, deep in the swamp.
26	A deep and murky lake in an underground cavern.	41	A series of brightly colored tents just outside the village, with a large open space for many people to gather.

D100	LOCATION	D100	LOCATION
42	On the deck of an airship during a sudden thunderstorm, while the captain tries to keep the ship sailing straight as it lists from thunder.	57	The bottom of a well that has gone dry with a tunnel leading off into darkness.
43	In the prison below the castle, locked in a plain stone cell with an iron door.	58	The kitchen of a fine bakery.
44	In the shadow of a giant sand dune that looks next to impossible to climb.	59	The king's royal chambers furnished with a beautiful curtained four-poster bed.
45	In the audience of the theater, in the upper row of boxes overlooking the stage.	60	The bunk room for the royal guard on the castle grounds.
46	On the lifeboat as the main ship sinks into the sea.	61	A long hallway that tilts slightly downward, that has also been greased with some sort of oil.
47	This forge is fueled by four great ovens that light up the blacksmith and her apprentices as they work.	62	A book of fables that, when opened, pulls its reader inside the stories.
48	A hunting lodge high up the mountainside overlooking a lush forested valley.	63	On a series of hastily stacked logs that span across a raging river and are slick with water.
49	An under-mountain grotto that is clearly a pirate's base of operations.	64	The beautifully manicured gardens of a high-ranking noble who is currently having a quiet social gathering.
50	The shipping docks of a very busy port with a merchant ship unloading its cargo.	65	In the middle of a giant bee's beehive with worker drones all around, but they don't yet seem to notice the players.
51	A scalding-hot arena. Magnified sunlight beams down everywhere. Burns will be quick and severe.	66	In the back alley of a row of buildings in the merchant district of town in the dark of night.
52	Deep within a mine shaft where the way out has just collapsed.	67	The large open-air marketplace around the fountain at the center of town.
53	In the vaults of the kingdom's treasury.	68	Locked to the wall in the torture room of the main villain's lair.
54	This 10- by 20-foot stone room is filled with piles of garbage and animal carcasses.	69	A narrow switchback trail that leads up the side of the mountain.
55	An out-of-place banquet room deep underground with settings and places for twenty people.	70	In the middle of a merchant caravan making its long journey across the scorching desert.
56	A well-lit study full of new parchment and ink, freshly laid rugs, and a warming fire.	71	A vast open prairie filled with long grass that comes up to a human's waist and is dotted with clumps of wildflowers.

D100	LOCATION	D100	LOCATION
72	A simple and unadorned one-room church with only a few pews and an altar.	87	The spiky bottom of a pit trap.
73	In the secret passages running through the castle walls that are often used as escape routes.	88	A dreamscape with strangely melting objects, otherworldly geography, and non-Euclidean geometry.
74	The chilly operating room of a necromancer's laboratory.	89	A castle sculpted out of plants, making it resemble a giant topiary. Flowers of all kinds mark which sections are actually doors.
75	The large common room of a roadside flophouse.	90	A 20- by 30-foot rectangular room with cracks all across the floor. Jets of hot steam or frigid air randomly shoot up out of a crack.
76	An area with a portal from the bottom of a 100-foot fall to the top of the area. The encounter is conducted in freefall.	91	The center of a large prison with entities attempting to break out of every cell.
77	A rocky forest area with geysers spraying boiling water every few minutes.	92	A serene, beautiful clearing near a lake. Cherry blossoms float on the breeze.
78	A mountain of gold being gradually sucked into a vacuous portal.	93	A house left alone for decades or perhaps centuries. Whispers of the past can be heard in the creaks of the floorboards.
79	The floor here is very sticky. It takes great effort to pry feet off the ground with each step.	94	The astral plane. Did the players die at some point and forget? No...that couldn't be right.
80	The eye of a hurricane. It moves slowly but surely, so characters will need to move with it or be swept up!	95	A cave slick with water from steam vents all around.
81	An impressively finished underground bunker seemingly built to withstand a doomsday event.	96	A temple of white marble with waterfalls pouring down its walls into a small river that flows to a basin in the center of the temple.
82	The base of a volcano with active lava flow. The lava gradually overtakes sections of solid ground.	97	A bunker built on the rim of the caldera of an active volcano. The heat is almost unbearable.
83	An underground research facility with foreign technology beyond the characters' understanding.	98	A tilted wizard's tower that is slowly sinking into the mud.
84	A mesa with small ledges leading up to the top.	99	A small village fully submerged in the water at the bottom of a lake.
85	A cliff wall. There are lots of good handholds, but the encounter is still strange and more vertical.	100	A large rock outcropping that is surrounded by sinkholes that randomly seem to appear.
86	A colosseum where high rollers bet big money on the outcomes of vicious fights.		

MONSTERS

The best way to think of a monster is as an NPC that can't talk. They populate your encounters and act both as characters in their own right and as obstacles. Whether you need an animal or an abomination, you can find it here.

D100	MONSTERS
1	A common animal, magically enlarged. Kind of cute at its normal size, horrifying at this macro level.
2	A lost dog in fight-or-flight mode.
3	A guardian spirit trying to prevent something from happening.
4	A talking cat that can cast devastating spells.
5	An enemy from the past returns with revenge in mind.
6	An ancient ghost obsessed with puzzles, riddles, and mazes.
7	A living building intent on scaring its inhabitants senseless.
8	A predator species hunting villagers of another species that is its natural prey.
9	A dark parallel of each member of the party that sees themselves as the superior set of rivals.
10	Tentacles that writhe through portals opening seemingly at random.
11	A bevy of skeletons in ancient-looking armor.
12	A mimic that gains control of flesh, then shapes it into horrifying weapons.

D100	MONSTERS
13	A town leader that brings the whole town guard to fight the party.
14	A huge bear whose eyes are completely gray. There are stalks of black goo coming out of its head.
15	A legion of usually insignificant foes rendered dangerous by sheer numbers.
16	It lives inside the shadows. It can be heard scratching and clawing but cannot be seen.
17	A restless spirit looking to avenge its death by killing anyone unlucky enough to disturb it.
18	A giant hybrid of wasp and spider with lots of wriggling babies on its back.
19	A small, furry creature that initially looks cute and innocent, but quickly reveals that it is extremely dangerous.
20	Animated statues of giants that stand motionless until a door is opened.
21	A mischievous unseen ghost that knocks random doors and walls, and mimics voices.
22	A monster tamer in command of a young red dragon, a vine wraith, and a lesser tortoise water elemental.
23	The ghosts of all the animals slaughtered for a nearby town's recent feast.
24	A pile of humanoid bodies grotesquely melting together. As they move, they collectively scream.
25	A changeling bent on ruining the reputation of one of the players.
26	A normally benevolent forest spirit that is angry at the players for disrespecting nature.
27	A horde of insects, worms, and arachnids forming into a vaguely humanoid shape.

D100	MONSTERS	D100	MONSTERS
28	The monster that lives in children's closets. It can create portals out of any doorway.	42	Humanoid lions in ornate armor wielding great swords.
29	Half of the party is temporarily rendered evil and attacks the rest of the characters.	43	A clockwork minotaur that uses golden spiked wires as a flail.
30	A mirror that shows awful things behind you. They aren't in the real world, but they can definitely hurt you.	44	An animated stone statue of an oversized lion.
31	It stalks, traps, and swallows its victims over the course of days or weeks.	45	Eight mud people that when destroyed merge into one giant mud blob that can create any type of appendage it needs.
32	A small demon-like entity that shows up from time to time to cause embarrassment.	46	A giant vine that sticks out of the ground that can shoot poisonous spikes from its lily-like flower.
33	A group of zombie dinosaurs that breaks through the ground.	47	A giant eyeball with wings and two clawed legs. It can physically stun any creature it sees in order to grab it and fly away.
34	The oldest troll that ever lived. Enormous, ancient, covered in scars, and wielding an immense club.	48	A small cluster of precious gems that uses a series of small tentacles to drag itself around. It explodes when hit, sending shards everywhere.
35	Land sharks that can somehow swim through the ground, tearing up anything in their path.	49	Three human-shaped beetles that have thick armored exoskeletons and vice-like mandibles.
36	A deserted town. All the buildings are actually intricate puppets that can be commanded to attack.	50	A walking tree that drools sap to trap foes, then plants them in the ground to be crushed by its roots.
37	A bevy of tiny fairies that look like they are wearing rose blooms as skirts or kilts. They flit around on gossamer wings and blow incapacitating dust into enemies' faces.	51	Six creatures that look like human children, but each of their heads is a different root vegetable. They are powerful burrowers and use various scents to incapacitate their enemies.
38	It retreats from sunlight. It's unbeatable in shadow.	52	A golden griffin and its flock.
39	Twenty-five porcelain dolls with razor-sharp claws.	53	A 15-foot-tall yeti with massive mammoth tusks and rows of sharp teeth.
40	A three-headed grizzly bear that's slightly larger than a normal bear.	54	A very small bear that is fond of riddles. If you can solve its puzzles, it will refrain from using its surprisingly deadly force.
41	A mass of limbs from random corpses stuck together, with one big eye in the center and a gaping maw below that eye.	55	A dryad in the shape of a saguaro cactus that dances around and shoots paralyzing needles.

D100	MONSTERS	D100	MONSTERS
56	A brooding elf with a razor whip and chewing gum.	70	Three balls of floating fire that can hurl parts of itself to cause an explosion on impact.
57	A flock of birds that are made out of pure light; they burn anything they land on or touch.	71	The captain of the royal guard and an expert marksman.
58	An enormous snake-like dragon that stays mostly underwater and uses bursts of water to push creatures off the land and into the water to be eaten.	72	A small straw doll that attempts to steal a player's hair and swallow it so that they are bonded. Any damage done to the doll is magnified back to the player.
59	Twenty frogmen who are excellent hunters with spears and swallow their prey whole to be digested over time.	73	Termites made completely out of water that re-form back to whole if struck poorly.
60	Animated ivy vines that take the shape of a dragon that likes to constrict its prey.	74	A set of twins, one of which is the evil twin. The players have a limited time to find out which is evil.
61	A seven-headed hydra that has two stumps where the other heads should be.	75	A huge termite eating a whole village's worth of houses.
62	An enraged chef who is an expert with the butcher's knife.	76	The mother of thousands of slugs that can take over minds.
63	Someone all the players know for certain is dead. They are acting mostly like they did in life, but slightly off.	77	A giant crab that is actually one hundred little crabs all linked together and acting as one.
64	It looks harmless, but is concealing its tremendous power and evil aura.	78	A demonic unicorn with a twisted dagger-like horn and flaming hooves.
65	A 10-foot-tall clockwork soldier in heavy armor and wielding an impossibly large sword.	79	He is feared across the land for his cruelty and killing prowess. His dark red armor is unmistakable, as is the barbed sword he wields.
66	A 2-foot-tall floating icicle that radiates extreme cold and is instinctively drawn to anything giving off heat.	80	Her face is made up like a skull; her armor is black as night. She is a master with two swords in her hands, and she moves like the wind.
67	A Frankenstein-like elf that has one arm that is a bear claw; the other arm is a crab claw.	81	Everything they touch burns, wilts, or withers. You can see their breath even on the warmest of days, but they give off no smell.
68	A human corpse with a parasitic bug sticking out of its stomach that allows the corpse to move and attack if needed.	82	Thirteen disembodied hands that scuttle into the shadows to hide and attack from safety.
69	A 30-foot-long crocodile with massive jaws and eight legs that make it able to move extremely fast.	83	Ants that swarm and bite, but they are also made of fire so they burn too.

D100	MONSTERS	D100	MONSTERS
84	The notorious thief named The Fading Light who has beaten the best locks in the world and whose face has never been seen.	93	A mass of goop that can transform into anything. It glows in the dark no matter what form it's in.
85	An opera singer with a voice so powerful that she can shatter metal.	94	A figure that seems to always be just in the background of every bad event.
86	A bard that can alter reality by the lyrics they sing.	95	A giant glob of flesh with a multitude of eyes and many sharp teeth.
87	She dances with ribbons that can cut like knives.	96	An unseen presence stalking the party from the shadows.
88	A local leader, presumed dead, who was transformed into a tentacled blob by an enemy.	97	Monsters that can perfectly mimic ordinary objects. Detectable only by touch.
89	He is at least 7 feet tall and every inch is covered in muscle. He holds a great axe in his right hand, and it almost looks like a toy.	98	A curse that follows the cursed individual in the form of a scary child. It appears from nowhere periodically to scare and do some harm to the cursed.
90	A gargantuan stone giant who fiercely and violently protects the child who accidentally summoned them.	99	A graceful swan that transforms into a hideous beast at the slightest disturbance.
91	They fight with no weapons and wear no armor, but their fists have never been defeated in any battle.	100	A room, that when entered, entraps the unlucky victim in a hallucinatory cycle of boring grunt work. The room is a monster that feeds on the despair of the trapped.
92	When someone buries treasure and leaves it for too long, wandering creatures can become fused to the cache of valuables, creating a treasure ghoul. These beings are very dangerous and want nothing more than to add to their mass of valuables by any means necessary.		

MOTIVATIONS

This table helps out when you've already introduced an NPC but you don't yet know **what drives them,** either in the moment or in their life. This is great when your players get more invested in a "throw-away" NPC than expected.

D100	MOTIVATIONS	D100	MOTIVATIONS
1	This being needs to eat a very specific item of food to be truly satisfied.	9	Believes they are under a curse of bad luck.
2	They desperately need medical attention in order to save their child.	10	They just want to see and catalog every animal in existence.
3	This character offers to buy a bard's lute, only to smash it to bits.	11	They can't just take the listed prices for anything; they always have to haggle.
4	They want to sell a cleric "miracle insurance" in case a healing goes wrong.	12	They believe every item they find, no matter how common, is magical.
5	This character makes decisions based only on money. No matter what, the highest bidder wins their loyalty.	13	They want to explore uncharted areas of the world, and are willing to pay for help to do so.
6	Information on a lost loved one will convince this person to do almost anything.	14	A fitness enthusiast who won't stop talking about their "every muscle" program.
7	Kill, kill, kill, kill, kill, kill, kill, kill, kill, *kill*!	15	They are dying of a slow-acting poison. Either a cure or bucket list items would be great.
8	Just wants to go back to bed.	16	They are looking to marry the most powerful person in the land for political gain.

D100	MOTIVATIONS	D100	MOTIVATIONS
17	They are pitting local leaders against each other, attempting to start a war.	31	They want blood samples (taken discreetly) from anyone they meet.
18	They feel the need to prove that they are the most talented spellcaster in the realm.	32	They have a powerful need to destroy a certain monster.
19	They've lost friends in battle and blame themself. They no longer allow close relationships.	33	They've made a Faustian bargain to be incredible at something but regret the awful price they had to pay.
20	Ravenous hunger has pushed them to the breaking point mentally.	34	Someone close to them is in danger, and they want very much to save them.
21	A god has commanded this individual to do something very out of the ordinary.	35	They are from far away and want to understand the customs of this place.
22	Needs to be in two different places at once tonight, and has a plan just zany enough to work.	36	It's their birthday, and on their birthday, they get *everything* they want!
23	A vampire who desperately wants to shed their curse before they forget all of their humanity.	37	They've heard so many heroic stories that it's inspired them to adventure!
24	Looking for donations to go toward a resurrection spell for their lost love.	38	They are carrying out the last wish of their dying parent.
25	Just loves riddles and will bug the players to tell one until they can't come up with an answer.	39	They are bored with their privileged life and feel that they need to be tested to prove their worth to society.
26	They've been given a large sum of money to commit a horrible act. They're conflicted but need the money.	40	They are being blackmailed by a secret that would cost them their life should it become public knowledge.
27	They can't stand any of the players, except one (chosen at random) that they are incredibly kind to.	41	They are searching for their one true love that they've only seen in a dream.
28	They're trying to solve a mystery and are eager to explain (in excruciating detail) all the clues they have so far.	42	They killed a witch when they were a child lost in the forest and now are bent on making sure all children are safe.
29	They believe they are cursed by local warlocks and want help ridding themself of the bad magic making them sick.	43	They claim that a wish split their soul into seven parts, and they are searching for the other six versions of themselves.
30	They cannot be reasoned with; even if their life is in danger, they are steadfast in their resolve.	44	They are the only survivor of a wizard battle that destroyed their home village and they are terrified of even the most benign magic trick.

D100	MOTIVATIONS	D100	MOTIVATIONS
45	As a child they could talk to all the animals but noticed that that ability faded as they grew. They desperately want to get that ability back.	60	As a child, a demon was bound within them, and they are constantly trying to do the right thing because they fear they are secretly evil.
46	They are trying to revive an ancient order of knights that they read about in a scroll but have found no other information about them yet.	61	They are obsessed with the players. They've made fan art and apparel, and have a scrapbook of news parchments.
47	They were banished from the kingdom when they pointed out that the king's new outfit was just a bunch of rags.	62	Starts out wanting to fight the players but can be reasoned with, perhaps even becoming a friend.
48	They feel deeply and duplicate the emotions of the people around them. They are searching for a place where people are at peace.	63	They want it all: fame, fortune, power. And they'll go to great lengths to achieve their goals.
49	They are plagued with visions of the world ending and are desperate to find a way to stop this from happening.	64	They want to be liked by everyone.
50	They have studied herbs all their life and feel they have nothing more to learn here. They need to travel.	65	Their family was killed by a devil and they are out for revenge!
51	They were rescued by their friends from a place they thought was paradise, and they need to find a way back.	66	They've taken on the mantle of the hero who died saving them, and now they need to keep that good name alive in the people's minds.
52	They were told by a fortune teller that they won't die until they are a ripe old age, so they are extremely reckless.	67	They are obsessed with control and controlling people, always subtly manipulating everyone around them.
53	They were raised by their far older brother after their parents disappeared mysteriously, a mystery they are driven to solve.	68	They will do anything to keep their hometown safe and hidden.
54	They were left on the doorstep of their parents by a zombie and need to know more about where they came from.	69	They lost a battle to their childhood rival and are now trying to better themself for when they meet again, perhaps for the last time.
55	They've grown up in school and feel that all of the books they've read have more than prepared them for life outside school grounds.	70	They have to keep taking jobs, no matter how risky, so they can support their family back home.
56	A prophecy told them they would be the greatest villain the world has ever known, and they are desperate to avoid that fate.	71	They are working off a debt of honor to a local lord, but they always seem to do something wrong that extends the debt.
57	They have a tragic backstory but they never seem to tell it the same way twice.	72	They want to be best friends with one of the players, but for nefarious reasons.
58	They say they were granted a wish and need to explore the world to make sure they make the best wish possible.	73	Insists that the players stay for a while until trouble passes.
59	They grew up in a forest city and really want to explore and live in an underground city.	74	Wants to cook and serve rare dishes.

D100	MOTIVATIONS	D100	MOTIVATIONS
75	They cheated on their entrance exam to the academy and need to prove themself while keeping that a secret.	88	They want to ensure that fighting doesn't ensue. They will go to great lengths to prevent conflict.
76	They freeze up whenever they have to make a decision, trying to calculate all the possible outcomes because they've made a very poor decision in the past.	89	They were kicked out of the academy for poor performance and now want to make a name for themself to rub it in their professors' faces.
77	They are searching for a long-lost civilization that they think holds the key to their family line.	90	They are keeping a huge secret that could destroy their life if discovered.
78	Their family expects them to be a knight like their father, grandfather, and great-grandfather, but they aren't so sure this is the life for them. Nevertheless, they feel they have to give it a good shot.	91	They say that this is their fourth chance at living and they are going to try to get it right this time. They do always seem to know what is going to happen next.
79	They feel that if they see the ocean, they will be drawn into it and changed fundamentally, so they avoid large bodies of water at all costs.	92	They think very highly of themself. They have unshakable (and unfounded) confidence.
80	They believe that ancient dragons can be reasoned with, and they become allies to any nation that tries so they can prove their theory.	93	They are living a new life in hiding from someone seeking revenge.
81	They have a crush on everyone but also are too nervous to be direct about it.	94	They are determined to kill a short list of people who wronged them.
82	They lie for no reason, and about almost everything. They love to deceive for deception's sake.	95	They are creating an encyclopedia of all creatures, monsters, gods, and other important entities in the world.
83	They run a local drug trade that is destroying lives.	96	They used to be a pirate captain but lost their ship and crew in an embarrassing incident.
84	They are in deep with a local cult but desperately want to get out.	97	They constantly need reassurance that they are okay and that you are okay.
85	They are actually an ancient evil waiting in disguise for an opportunity to take over the world.	98	They have never been defeated and are always looking for worthy rivals.
86	They are a sweet elderly person who wants to know how you're doing and to give you candy.	99	They're trying to get a group together for a job with a huge potential payout.
87	They always want to be on the underdog's team. They will change alliance if one group begins dominating.	100	They're a bard looking for their next big hit. They've run out of inspiration.

MAGIC EFFECTS

Magic is one of the coolest narrative perks of setting your story in a fantasy world, and this table provides one hundred fascinating magical effects great for everything from consumable spell scrolls or magic traps, to powerful reusable artifacts.

D100	MAGIC EFFECTS	D100	MAGIC EFFECTS
1	All surfaces in the realm of influence are extremely bouncy. Characters can't even take a step without being hurled into the air.	9	At the start of the encounter, everyone randomly teleports 10 feet.
2	Combat noises are replaced with squeaky toy sounds.	10	Everyone is blinded by sudden, random flashes of light.
3	Everyone turns invisible.	11	A wizard passing by casts time-stopping magic on the whole encounter so they can pass by without issue.
4	The floor is literally lava.	12	Each character is body-swapped into another character.
5	For some reason, all spells backfire here.	13	Every hit results in a small explosion.
6	Everyone gains extra armor in one form or another.	14	The members of the encounter shrink to the size of a lima bean.
7	Any metal in the encounter becomes brittle.	15	Everyone transforms into the first creature they think of.
8	Vines appear everywhere and try to wrap anyone they touch.	16	Magical fog makes characters unable to see more than a few feet in front of them.

D100	MAGIC EFFECTS	D100	MAGIC EFFECTS
17	An anti-magic field renders all other magic useless.	32	Everyone manifests an aura companion: an animal friend made of your personal energy.
18	All characters are compelled to sing about what they are doing.	33	All melee attacks create an energy burst that travels up to 100 feet away.
19	Fireballs rain down at regular intervals, telegraphing where they will land with bull's-eyes on the ground.	34	Torches and other light sources suddenly provide darkness rather than light.
20	Everyone can fly for the duration of this encounter.	35	Everything is a different color than normal.
21	All sound is magically stopped. Nothing can make a sound here.	36	All characters have enhanced strength inversely correlated to their normal strength compared to the others.
22	The cat got everyone's tongue. Players may only communicate with meows.	37	All spells target the caster and their target at the same time. If the target is the caster, then it randomly affects another target.
23	Everyone feels mirrored pain when they inflict it on others.	38	Something terrible happens, killing all the players! Suddenly, time reverses and they are able to try again.
24	Everything goes dark. The only time anyone can see anything is when it moves.	39	All elemental spells cast are suddenly their opposite element. Fire becomes water, air become earth, and vice versa.
25	All characters are duplicated. The duplicates have opposite motivations of their original.	40	Everyone can choose to see through another creature's eyes, including friends and enemies.
26	All characters have speed-enhancing magic, meaning they take double the normal actions.	41	Gravity stops working for the duration of the encounter. Everyone floats and needs to propel themselves to move.
27	The ground changes elevation in waves across the landscape, going from 0 to 30 feet higher.	42	Everyone must speak out loud the name of the spell they are casting, anime style.
28	In this encounter, everyone can read each other's minds, and may find information they'd rather not.	43	The caster's skin turns a color matching the type of spell they just cast. Red for fire, green for air, etc.
29	Everyone is rendered extremely sleepy. If they don't move their full movement each turn, they fall asleep.	44	Harmless apparitions appear all over the battlefield in random places, often blocking lines of sight.
30	"I don't know" is a magical phrase that strikes the speaker with a small but painful jolt of electricity.	45	Everyone's weapon gets a random enchantment for one minute.
31	Everything looks extremely stylized and cute. Have everyone describe what their character looks like under the effects of this cartoon character spell.	46	Spells can only be cast if the name of the spell is said out loud and backward.

D100	MAGIC EFFECTS	D100	MAGIC EFFECTS
47	All metal armor becomes like a magnet, making it easier to be hit by other metal objects.	62	The gravity of this place shifts to 50 percent of what it was.
48	Everyone becomes insubstantial, allowing them to pass through objects and reduce the damage from attacks from weapons.	63	Words of encouragement are given real power. Any genuine compliment given bestows a magical bonus to the compliment receiver.
49	Everyone can choose one enemy to target that mystically becomes easier to hit, but the enemies will get the same advantage.	64	Sparks shoot from everyone in the vicinity. No one can sit still for forty-eight hours.
50	Everyone gets a clone they can control, and everyone gets one turn for each version of themselves.	65	Everything and everyone here ages ten years.
51	Any spell has enhanced power if the user utters a rhyming couplet beforehand.	66	Everyone nearby is hypnotized and susceptible to suggestions.
52	No one here can die. Any mortal wounds happen, and hurt, but are then reversed.	67	The effect creates a magical automaton. It's almost alive, and resents its existence.
53	Glitter sprays out of all casters' hands whenever they cast a spell.	68	A weapon gains sentience. It is pretty dumb.
54	A pink dust floats in the air. Touching it creates a feeling of joy. It's hard to do anything but feel happy.	69	Someone reflexively casts a spell at random.
55	One of everyone's limbs seems possessed for this encounter. The limb moves fitfully all on its own.	70	This effect carves out magical scars in someone. They are like regular scars, but translucent and glowing.
56	This encounter seems to exist in a temporal bubble. Time is passing by at a different speed outside.	71	A line of communication opens up to the Source. It is perplexed at being called like this.
57	Most words become power-infused. "Fire" results in a fire spell; "Duck!" results in a duck being created; etc.	72	Everyone in the encounter is transported 174 hours into the future.
58	Your hand has started glowing blue every time it rains.	73	Everyone swells with magical energy mimicking physical muscle. The gains are relative to one's confidence.
59	Your spell accidently turned a nearby cat into a person who won't stop stalking you down the road.	74	Someone is transported to the realm of the dead.
60	Someone can speak only in rhyme now. Unless what they say is a rhyming couplet, they cannot speak.	75	Someone involuntarily astral projects and cannot return to their body.
61	Your head begins to hurt more and more painfully the longer you go without casting a spell. The pain can become debilitating.	76	Someone is compelled to follow the orders of another character in the encounter.

D100	MAGIC EFFECTS	D100	MAGIC EFFECTS
77	Everyone here is now under the effect of a rage spell. They are so mad.	89	Everyone suddenly grows an animal tail of their choice.
78	Someone's connection to the source of their power is severed.	90	Someone grows gills and can now breathe only in water.
79	Casting anything other than the most basic spells makes the caster violently sick; the stronger the spell, the more sick they feel. Only those with a strong constitution will avoid throwing up.	91	The caster's method of casting magic has become damaged, and now they never know exactly which spell will come out. But it will be surprisingly powerful.
80	Something begins pulsing at faster and faster intervals. It will explode with magic energy soon.	92	The caster can spit acid for the next three hours.
81	The strange magic enables *something* from another realm to possess someone.	93	You can now see perfectly in complete darkness but can't see anything if there is bright light.
82	Someone is transformed into their infant self.	94	You can understand everything animals say, but you can't understand any humanoid language.
83	Someone's arms and legs grow four times longer.	95	Every spell cast is suddenly on a time delay going off 1d6 turns later.
84	The veil above is lifted. Characters are made aware that they are characters in a role-playing game.	96	Everyone's hair falls out and then suddenly grows back in a completely different and unusual color.
85	All the air nearby is transformed into water.	97	The caster gains x-ray vision and is able to see everyone's skeleton.
86	Magically putrid smells erupt.	98	Everyone's shadows come to life and start attacking them.
87	Friction is removed from objects nearby.	99	The caster's eyes turn completely black for the next week, but their vision is not affected. People just find them scary now.
88	Everyone loses the ability to see color. Everything is in black and white.	100	Your current task magically completes.

WILD CARD

Even the coolest encounter can get stale if it doesn't keep you on your toes! This table is filled with **surprises, lucky breaks, and complications** that are designed to give encounters an extra kick. These work best when you roll them in the middle of play.

D100	WILD CARD	D100	WILD CARD
1	In the middle of the encounter, a character is grabbed and held at crossbow-point. A standoff ensues.	9	An explosion nearby interrupts this encounter halfway through.
2	An earthquake interrupts the encounter and splits the ground between two halves of the party.	10	Someone in the party is offered a compelling reason to betray the others.
3	An object everyone wants is completely destroyed before anyone has time to use it.	11	An enemy has a change of heart and switches sides.
4	A magical being transports the party outside space and time to prove why their reality should be saved.	12	A massive flock of birds interrupts the encounter, swarming everyone.
5	An intense storm crackles overhead, drenching everything and booming with intense lightning.	13	Something the players knew for sure is revealed to be false.
6	The usual, reliable source of light is suddenly compromised. The encounter is much darker than anticipated.	14	A fire starts at the beginning of the encounter and gradually spreads as time passes.
7	The party is very tired. The last few days have been tougher than they thought, and they are exhausted.	15	A new faction is introduced that hates all other parties involved in the encounter.
8	Someone from the past shows up to demand something.	16	A secret long held is suddenly revealed to everyone.

D100	WILD CARD	D100	WILD CARD
17	An injury is more extreme than it first appears and leaves the wounded with a permanent reminder.	31	The light here is extremely harsh. When not in shadow, characters are burned.
18	A child chases a ball into the middle of the encounter.	32	This encounter turns into a contest of strength of some kind. One contestant on each side will compete.
19	The reason for the encounter is revealed to be a false assumption.	33	The air here has a particle that sparks an allergic reaction in one or more of the characters.
20	A stampede of wild boars suddenly rips through the area.	34	One of the characters has to go to the bathroom badly. It is an emergency. They need to find a way to discreetly leave the encounter.
21	A fireworks display is happening nearby. Everything is hard to see except during the explosions.	35	An integral person or part of this encounter is suddenly gone.
22	Something huge shatters in the playing field. Now, moving hurts anyone traveling on the ground.	36	Something that was calm suddenly goes out of control.
23	Everything here is a mimic. *Everything.*	37	Everyone is suddenly cool and more open to talking things through.
24	The players are swept up into a stranger's bachelorette party.	38	There is no way past this encounter without losing someone in the party.
25	The players stumble into a sudden sinkhole.	39	You are actually in space and on a different planet.
26	Rather than a fight, the current antagonist requests a game of whatever the players agree to.	40	For this encounter, everything is settled with a game of rock-paper-scissors.
27	Communication is impaired. The players must secretly explain to the GM what they do on their turns. The players cannot communicate with each other.	41	For this encounter, dice are not allowed. Everyone must report how their character *feels* about their attack, then the GM decides how it goes.
28	Something forces a change of scenery. All characters move to another map.	42	Music should be played during this encounter, and everyone needs to try their best to talk on beat.
29	This encounter is two-dimensional. Characters can only move left or right, or jump/climb up and down.	43	Plans change because someone can no longer perform a task.
30	A toxic gas is released into the area. Anyone breathing the poison air is hurt.	44	If an insane plan that should not work is suggested during this encounter, it miraculously works!

D100	WILD CARD	D100	WILD CARD
45	The weather changes dramatically and quickly.	60	A crowd of people begins flooding into the area.
46	The players realize they are in a shared dream.	61	The longer this encounter goes on, the more they lose.
47	New evidence is presented that sheds doubt on something important.	62	Someone everyone thought was dead shows up with a dramatic entrance.
48	The encounter is rendered much easier through apathy.	63	Someone attempts to flee the area.
49	Something happens to split the party.	64	The area begins flooding at an alarming rate.
50	Each player suddenly has something they need to deal with before they can help the rest of the group.	65	The stakes of the encounter are dramatically raised.
51	It is revealed that something here is contagious. If the players come in direct contact, they risk exposure.	66	Someone very powerful sends an agent after the players.
52	If anyone panics here, it could lead to everyone dying.	67	A trusted ally betrays the players but clearly doesn't want to.
53	The players are thrown into the future!	68	If an insane plan that should not work is suggested during this encounter, it miraculously works!
54	Find the least appropriate music for the situation and play it during this encounter.	69	Someone reveals a secret that gives them an extreme advantage here.
55	The next NPC the party meets will be an old friend from a player character's teen years.	70	Someone abruptly confesses their feelings.
56	Today just sucks, y'know? Everyone should complain loudly about whatever injuries their character gets.	71	A time limit is imposed on the encounter.
57	If anyone calls on a god for any power or even as an exclamation, they show up in person.	72	Someone changes their mind about something important.
58	Take a break to bake something. You deserve a treat!	73	A king or queen travels into the encounter along with their royal guard.
59	Turn the lights off, light a candle, and make this session more horror themed.	74	It's very distracting.

D100	WILD CARD	D100	WILD CARD
75	An old foe reappears!	88	Bullet time is in place. All attacks slow, allowing anyone a chance to dodge them, but otherwise time is normal.
76	This encounter should be completed without dice. Everyone should describe their actions. They happen just as described, as long as the other players agree.	89	Roll your attack dice ten times before the encounter starts and record those results. For the next encounter, those results are used once in any order.
77	For this encounter, each player gets assigned a character they don't normally play. They must do their best to act and make decisions like that character.	90	When rolling a die for an attack, if the number is even, the attack damage is doubled; if it is odd, the attack damage is halved for the duration of the encounter.
78	Initiative runs in reverse order for this next encounter.	91	Plant something together as a group (in the real world). As long as the plant survives, the group gets a small teamwork bonus.
79	Choose a player at random. Their character gets a boost of motivation, giving them the ability to reroll their next roll if they like. Ask the player what they think is on the character's mind that's motivated them.	92	Everyone takes a trip into their weapon, spellbook, or holy symbol and meets some creature that represents that item. If they can defeat them or partner with them, that weapon gains an appropriate enchantment.
80	Official observers of the kingdom arrive to measure and evaluate the players' performance to report back to the ruling council.	93	No one the players talk to takes them seriously.
81	Everyone place your bets on who will have the highest or lowest roll of the night.	94	A rival shows up to lend unexpected help, but states that the players now owe them one.
82	The temperature suddenly drops and it's snowing and sleeting. Everything is covered in a thin layer of ice and snow. Careful, it's slippery.	95	A player acting alone while in this encounter will always fail. The players must find creative ways of working together to be able to complete any task, including attacking.
83	It's min-max day. All positives, like people's attributes, are doubled, but so are all negatives.	96	Something can unexpectedly fly, taking this encounter to the sky.
84	Vines appear everywhere and try to wrap around anyone they touch.	97	Something unbelievable that one of the players thought might be the reason behind something actually is.
85	Everyone should come as a low-budget cosplay of their character next session.	98	Turn order is determined by whoever speaks up first. Everyone still gets the same number of turns.
86	Any sudden movements near it could result in an explosion.	99	Everyone chooses a chess piece and has to move on the battle map like that chess piece. There can only be one queen.
87	Bandits secretly watch this scene, ready to strike when the opportunity is right.	100	Someone left something important at home.

PART THREE

DOWNTIME

The most fun RPG campaigns are the ones where the group is able to pace the action well. As fun as non-stop action can be, eventually it's just exhausting. These downtime encounters are meant for those moments in your RPG where you need a break in the action.

Some of these are event-based encounters just like you'd see elsewhere in the book, but many others in this list read more like conversation prompts. That's because any time the characters rest as a group is a perfect time for group dialogue scenes. They let characters reflect on recent story events, define their relationships with the other characters, and flesh out their personalities.

REAL STORIES

Downtime encounters humanize the characters. We see them as heroes, but seeing them as just regular people is key to a good story. With that in mind, try to keep the events relatively open-ended. The plot you planned to close the encounter with, for instance, is likely less of a priority during downtime than letting the in-character banter lead the flow of the session conversationally.

For those reasons, these options are often heavy on the "role-playing" part of "role-playing game," but that's what you're here for anyway, isn't it? Embrace your inner theater person. It'll be fun!

D100	REAL STORIES
1	The characters decide to play an RPG. Which character GMs? What kind of character do the other PCs play as? Your current GM should play as an NPC with the group, so they aren't left out!
2	Let's play a drinking game! Act out what ensues. Who gets too drunk? Does anyone abstain? Who wins? What gets discussed in their inebriated state?
3	Conversation shifts to what the players would do if they won the Giga-Gold lottery.
4	The players have a meeting in the forest near town with an NPC from earlier in their adventures. The NPC is late. Quite late, in fact. And you can hear howling, but it doesn't quite sound like wolves. A pack of werewolves is dragging the NPC contact back to their den for dinner.
5	The group decides to play cards. Have a scene where we find out who wins big, who's out first, who doesn't understand the rules, and maybe even who cheats!

6	During a strange, shared dream, the players are visited by a figure in a blue cloak using a pick-axe to break open a cloud the color of midnight. They introduce themself as the Wodgian Wizard of the Weary. They need to extract people's nightmares in order to fuel their ongoing dream experiments. If desired, each player should describe their worst nightmare. Then, have a combat encounter where all of the nightmares come true. If the players are victorious, the wizard gives the players a card with their picture on it. This card can be used to cast a spell that summons a target's nightmare to attack them.
7	The players are getting on each other's nerves. What has irritated them, and how do the players compromise to help each other and make up?
8	The last scrape the players were in was a bit too close. Everyone seems on edge. How does everyone cope with their dangerous lifestyle? How do they support each other in these scary moments?
9	The players decide to tell ghost stories around a campfire. Which player has the best story? Who has the worst story? Who has the scariest story?
10	Already on edge, the players discover that the food bag has a hole in it, and over the course of the day most of the food has fallen out. Hungry, tired, and frustrated, will the players stay up to hunt for food or go to bed hungry?
11	Nearby, a group of athletes organizes an impromptu race into the headwinds of the biggest storm of the year, which approaches quickly. No vehicles are allowed, but roughhousing, spellcasting, and traps are encouraged.
12	The players all talk about where they live (when not adventuring) and why they live there.
13	In a moment of rest and friendship, the players get in a bit of an oversharing mood. What secrets do they divulge to the group?
14	The players are all up past normal bedtime, unable to rest. It's suggested, to help relax the group, that everyone tells of a historic event they've witnessed.
15	A peddler of illicit substances approaches the group and offers bottles of concoctions they claim will "loosen the muscles and expand the mind." Do any of the players partake? Do any abstain? The players should describe their experience, no matter what they chose.
16	Everyone decides it's a good time to work on their weaknesses. What does each player perceive as their weakness? Does the group agree? What will they do to work on it?
17	The players all realize it's Letters Day, the day when everyone throughout the land takes a moment to send a message to a loved one. Who does each player write to? What do they write?
18	The players have a chance encounter with a celebrity bard. Who is the biggest fan? Who has never heard of them?

D100	REAL STORIES
19	While the group sleeps, they have a collective dream visit to an ethereal playhouse. They are playing the parts of all of the actors but don't have any lines. The audience stares deeply and menacingly into the players' very souls. It seems they'll need to put on a show to avoid the crowd's backlash.
20	The subject of life partners comes up. What is each character looking for in a partner? Do they want kids? What does life after adventure look like for them?
21	One of your party's magic items gains sentience overnight! As the item develops a sense of self, each player chooses a flashback to an event the item was present for, and the players decide together how that event might have impacted the item's personality.
22	Sharing stories over a meal, each player regales the group with a story of their defining moment.
23	An NPC friend you haven't seen in quite some time got a promotion while you were gone! They invite the players as well as some of their own friends out for drinks to celebrate.
24	The group begins discussing music. What is each character's favorite genre? Favorite song? Favorite bard? Do any of the characters play an instrument or have any other musical training?
25	The group decides to play a sport. Maybe one of the players knows one, or maybe they make something up. What is the sport? What are the teams? Act out a scene exploring how the game goes.
26	Thoughts turn to a base of operations. Where does the team usually meet? How do they make that place their own? Do they have aspirations of a larger place all to themselves? What does the group's perfect adventuring lair look like?
27	There is a spectacular meteor shower tonight. Everyone is transfixed by the incredible show the cosmos is putting on. The group begins talking about hopes for the future. What does each character want *beyond* adventuring?
28	One of the players suggests telling everyone's fortunes. If anyone in the group knows any kind of fortune-telling technique, act it out for each character. If not, make something up!
29	The group collectively sniffs their clothes and realizes it's time for new duds. What is each character's new outfit?
30	One of the characters realizes, with a bit of surprise, that today is their birthday. How do the other characters make them feel special today?
31	There's a long enough span of time that the players take up small jobs to get a little extra coin. What does each character do for their side hustle?
32	As the players are relaxing by a campfire, cloaked figures on horseback gallop through the campsite, grabbing as many bags as they can and speeding away!

33	The group decides to have a secret gift-giving day. Everyone is assigned someone else to get a gift for. What does everyone choose to give?
34	The group is invited to dinner at the estate of a wealthy individual they saved recently. The dinner is very awkward, as it seems this person is intent on keeping the adventurers as live-in bodyguards.
35	Everyone is bored and decides to take up some hobbies. What is each character's passion outside of adventuring? What do they do or create?
36	All Hallows' Eve draws near, and the players have been invited to a costume ball! Who dresses up? How does the evening play out?
37	It's Feasting Day, but all they have to celebrate are their standard rations. Each member of the group is tasked with finding and preparing ingredients to make one dish for the players' feast. Have a scene with each character's journey to make their dish.
38	Since there's nothing to do tonight, the group decides to go to a local dance advertised on posters nearby.
39	The group isn't 100 percent sure, but the stars look to be in the right place for the annual Hiding Festival. Who is "it" for this highly venerated and serious game of hide-and-seek? Where and how do the characters hide? Who is found last?
40	As the sun sets and a new constellation is visible in the sky, the players realize tonight is the last day of the year. Have each character list their accomplishments this year and what they hope for in the new year.
41	Someone from the group's past sends a thank-you gift. Together, discuss who sent the gift, what the gift was, and why they felt the need to send it now.
42	The players decide to take advantage of this downtime and do some training. How does each character hone their skills? Appropriate experience should be awarded to each character based on their activity.
43	It's Spirit Week, meaning the veil between the world of the living and the world of the dead is thin, and people can visit their lost loved ones. Who does each character visit? What is the conversation like?
44	The group wakes up trapped in a strange spirit realm. They can see themselves through a mirror. Only it isn't them...they've been possessed!
45	Tonight, the subject of conversation is heroes. Who is each character's hero? What are they like? Why do they look up to this figure?
46	It's an extra cold night. What do the characters do to keep warm? Can anyone stand the cold? Is anyone more sensitive to chills?
47	The characters decide to play truth or dare. Have one round with each character choosing one and the group deciding what the truth or dare is. Consequences for refusing to answer or perform the dare should be decided by the players.

D100	REAL STORIES
48	A bard comes upon the group and asks if they know any good stories. If someone in the group can explain their story so far (in character), the bard reacts very favorably and promises to immortalize their story in song.
49	The party decides to play capture the flag. Divide the characters into teams and role-play the game together. Make sure each team is able to share information discreetly so they can make plans.
50	The players have sparring matches to hone their skills. Pair up randomly or choose who fights who. All damage is nonlethal for these fights, so go all out!
51	The characters shop for supplies. What does every character think of as "essential"? How much does everyone spend? Does anyone buy anything frivolous?
52	The party travels to the beach for a relaxing day on the shore. What is the day like? Role-play a "day off" for these characters. What kind of treats and meals do they eat? What kind of outfits do they wear? Who gets sunburned?
53	The players have a night of singing their favorite songs. What is each character's favorite song? Do they get up to sing it? Who dances? Who plays the songs? Why are these songs important to the characters?
54	The players opt to go to a "haunted house" for a laugh, but find it is an actually haunted house with undead monsters lurking behind every corner.
55	The players must say goodbye to someone or something that has been with them for a long while. Discuss as a group who or what is leaving and why. How do the characters say goodbye? How do they feel about this farewell?
56	Today is a magnificent day. This downtime is completely ideal for all the players. Have everyone explain their character's lovely day they had today.
57	One of the party members has scored front-row tickets to a superfamous bard that's making an appearance nearby! Together, create this bard idol's identity, then tell how the concert goes. Who has a great time? Who thinks it was a waste of time? Who gets merch?
58	It's a solemn day today. The players are attending a funeral for someone recently departed. Who is the deceased? What did they mean to each character? How does the funeral go?
59	One of the character's previous love interests arrives demanding what they are "owed." They seem deeply hurt and angry about the ending of the relationship. Whose ex is this? Have a scene with these two.
60	One of the characters receives word that they need to head home as soon as possible. Where is home? Are the other characters willing to go as well? Are they invited? What is the occasion?
61	Everyone wakes with a start. They forgot to study for the big exam! The exam is a fight with a legion of terrible nightmare creatures. To make things worse, they've forgotten their gear, coming to school today in only their underwear!

62	A storm threatens to ruin the players' rest. Upon further inspection, this storm is sentient! It's a storm elemental, and it's being a real jerk, disturbing nearby sleeping villages on purpose.
63	Calls for help can be heard far away. If the players investigate, they find an abandoned house is the source of the sounds. Someone has been locked in the basement by the sinister spirits that spend their afterlives tormenting anyone they can lure inside.
64	All the players have caught the bug that's been going around. It's not a dangerous illness, but the group needs to find somewhere to rest and recover. Describe their care routines when they are sick.
65	It's a dreary day today. Cold rain means staying outside is not a fun prospect. What do the players do to keep warm and stay occupied inside on this lazy day?
66	It's the party's anniversary! How long have they been together? How have the group's dynamics changed? Spend some time reminiscing about the past.
67	A rival adventuring party challenges the players to a game of kickball. Have a "combat" encounter where everyone uses any abilities they want to excel at this children's sport. Winner gets bragging rights as the best adventuring group around.
68	A nearby town is holding a bake-off with a prize of a huge stash of delicious food that sounds a *lot* more delicious than the players' rations. If the players decide to compete, what do they make? How does the contest go?
69	The players decide it's time for a vacation away from work. Where do they decide to go? For how long? What do they plan to do? Is one of the characters a big planner?
70	The group begins to discuss what keeps them together. Not just why they allied in the first place, but why they continue to travel and adventure together. Have each character describe their reasons for staying with the group.
71	Everyone seems to be in a foul mood today. What has the players down? Have a scene of each character's attempts to deal with their feelings today.
72	An echo-egress opens spontaneously where the players are resting. Collectively, the party can contact one person any distance away. Another egress opens near that person, and they can have a five-minute conversation.
73	The players watch the sunset together. The group shares stories as they look at the beautiful horizon. Have a scene where each character reveals something new about their past.
74	It's a full moon and the stars are shining abnormally bright. It's messed up everyone's sleep. What do the players do rather than get their rest tonight?
75	The players are invited to a wedding! Whose wedding is it? What do their wedding outfits look like? Role-play a few scenes of the wedding and the reception.

D100	REAL STORIES
76	One of the players realizes they have misplaced something very important to them. What is missing? Who misplaced it? Role-play the search and how the missing item is found.
77	The players begin talking about what they will do after this adventure is over. Do they intend to keep hanging out? Go on further adventures? Retire? What does the future look like for each character?
78	The players discuss who among them is objectively the strongest. Role-play the discussion. Who is most passionately involved in the discussion? Who is outraged? Who is sitting this one out?
79	The players are having a conversation about what they absolutely will *not* do for a mission. What is everyone's limit? Would anything ever change their mind? Why is that their limit?
80	The players' daydreams seem to be coming to life today. Have scenes with everyone experiencing this imagination déjà vu. What did they daydream about? How did the real version pan out?
81	The players talk about where they'd like to visit if they ever had the chance. Role-play each character's travel aspirations. Do they actually have a plan for how they will visit?
82	The players have a huge fight resulting in everyone taking some time away on their own. What do they disagree about? What does each character do on their own?
83	Everyone is tired of road rations. The players decide to have a cook-off. Each character will collect ingredients to make a dish that will impress the whole group.
84	Everyone is stressed out and needs to take some time dedicated to self-care. What does each character do to rejuvenate themself? Does the group do something relaxing together?
85	A person or group that the players have helped expresses their gratitude. Who is this grateful party, and what do they do? Is it received well by the characters?
86	The players are a bit bored and decide to get extremely into something. They want to make a large structure or piece of artwork or something. What does the group make? How do they make it? How does it turn out?
87	It's a good day for friendship. Have each player act out a scene with any other character where something positive happens. What happens? How do these characters grow closer?
88	A familiar face shows up having done something terrible and asking for the players' help. How is this person received? What did they do? What will the players do?
89	It's Teaching Day, a day celebrated throughout the land where everyone shares their skills with friends and family. Have a scene with each character teaching the others. What do they teach? Are they happy to educate? Are they a good teacher?

90	The tavern advertises a strange scavenger hunt. All the items seem to be spell ingredients, but the prize is pretty great. But why would someone need all of these ingredients?
91	The party plays two truths and a lie. Role-play each character's turn stating three facts about themselves, two of which are true and one of which is a lie. All of them can be made up on the spot, but two are now true about the character.
92	The players opt for a board game to pass the time. Pick out and play a real board game, but role-play and make decisions as your character. The GM can play any NPC so they can join in as well!
93	This time of year has all the characters thinking about their childhood. What are some things people remember from growing up? Even the worst backstories can have a moment of joy to look back upon, while otherwise unblemished childhoods can be marked by a single traumatic event.
94	The players realize it's been a while since any of them got in a really good cuddle with a friendly pet. They go in search of a pet rescue that could use some help and spend the day doing odd jobs in exchange for getting to play with all the wonderful animals up for adoption. Perhaps one of them would even make a good road companion....
95	One morning around the fire, the characters get a whiff of something a bit...off. They spend an embarrassing amount of time looking for stray bits of rotten food before realizing it's been quite some time since they were at a proper inn. With clothes washers and hot baths. Still, it was fun discovering long-forgotten items in the bottom of their packs.
96	In all the excitement of their recent endeavors, the characters begin to feel they are neglecting their more mundane skills. Does anyone have hobbies, or are they more focused on only things that can help them in the next fight?
97	A wandering bard joins the players at the campfire and tells them that he knows a fun way to pass the time by casting a magical ritual. He will play a song and through the magic, a series of dance steps will appear on the ground. It's the players' job to keep up with the dance steps without missing a beat.
98	The players' success and fame has spread throughout the city, and they are being courted by a number of guilds who would like them to join to raise their stature. What guilds interest the players? What do they want to get out of joining a guild? What do they want to learn from a guild if they do join?
99	A famous dwarven brewery wants to honor the players by making a special ale named after them. What's the ale's name? What flavors go into it? How common or uncommon are the ingredients?
100	A gnomish inventor wants to honor the players by making automated action figures of them. What does the figure do? What armor or outfits do you choose? How closely does the figure look like them? Does it come with a lot of accessories?

ABOUT THE AUTHORS

The authors of this book are also the creators and hosts of *Very Random Encounters*, a random-generation-filled actual-play RPG podcast you can find at VRE.show.

Travis "Wheels" Wheeler (they/them) has discovered an ancient magical artifact that allows them to add an extra twelve hours into every day, just enough extra time to make multiple weekly podcasts and act as behind-the-scenes editor for many more, including *Interstitial* and *Got it Memorized*? They live in chilly Winnipeg, Manitoba, Canada, but hail from the slightly less chilly Muskegon, Michigan, USA.

Logan Jenkins (he/him) helps edit, create music, and make art and designs for the podcast. He lives in Greenville, South Carolina, with his boyfriend, where he has a whole bookcase devoted to RPG books, and wishes he had more time to play them all.

Lee Terrill (she/her) hasn't met an RPG yet that she doesn't like. Her main hobby, outside of gaming, is mostly collecting other hobbies, but you can also find her every week on the podcast *Very Random Encounters*, where she plays many diverse characters with extremely similar southern accents. She lives in Greenville, South Carolina, with her husband and their incredibly needy cat, The Stig.

Greg Leatherman (he/him) graduated with a degree in theater arts, and he's put all those skills into bringing characters to life in his favorite pastime: playing Tabletop RPGs and self-publishing his own award-winning RPG called *Glitter Hearts* in 2020. You can hear him on many other podcasts, like *Mythical* and *It's Super Effective*. He lives in Minneapolis with his husband and two dogs, fending off the cold winters.

You can find the authors rolling dice for actual play podcasts on the randomly generated *Very Random Encounters* or the ambitious crossover event podcast and official audio companion to the RPG system that shares its name, *Interstitial*.

They also take on the herculean task of recapping the plot of the Kingdom Hearts and Final Fantasy video games on the comedy recap show *Got It Memorized*?

Imagine how little free time they'd have if they actually had to do all that *and* hold down a full-time day job without time magic!

ABOUT THE ILLUSTRATORS

Rob Donovan was born in Essex but now resides in West Wickham, Kent (UK), where he lives with his wife, three sons (no more!), and a King Charles Spaniel called Scout. He attained a degree in ancient history from the University of Kent in 2000. Rob began writing and illustrating seriously in 2010, and to date has published seven novels and commissioned more than 150 maps. You can find his work on his website, RobDonovanAuthor.com. Rob is also proud to be legally classed as the Lord of Tattingstone, Tattingstone being a square meter of grass situated in a muddy field in the north of England.

Cinta (Cinthia) Rashford is a graphic designer from Spain. She was born in the small eastern city of Les Roquetes, about 100 miles south along the coast from Barcelona, in 1999. She studied art and design at the Escola d'Art i Disseny d'Amposta (ESARDI) in Amposta, Spain. She currently works as a freelance illustrator.

INDEX

THE
ULTIMATE
BOOKS
FOR THE
ULTIMATE
CAMPAIGN!

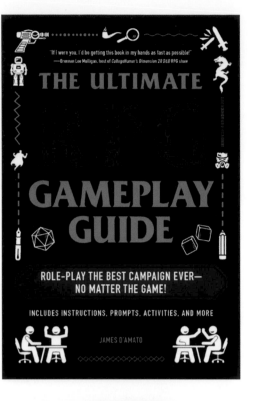

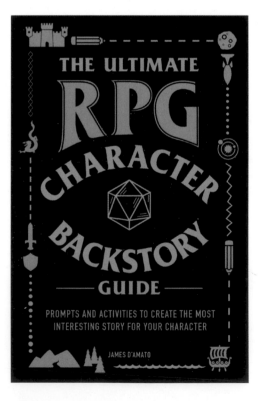